Detector Dogs, Dynamite Dolphins,

and more animals with

Super Sensory Powers

Detector Dogs, Dynamite Dolphins,

AND MORE ANIMALS WITH

Super Sensory Powers

Christina Couch *and* **Cara Giaimo**

illustrations by **Daniel Duncan**

mit Kids Press

To Mom, Jason, and Lillian,
the best partners for exploring this amazing world
CC

To Peppercorn and Poppyseed,
who will never work a day in their lives
CG

• • •

The MIT Press, the ☰**mit Kids** Press colophon, and MIT Kids Press are trademarks of The MIT Press,
a department of the Massachusetts Institute of Technology, and used under license from The MIT Press.
The colophon and MIT Kids Press are registered in the US Patent and Trademark Office.

First edition 2022

Library of Congress Catalog Card Number 2021953118
ISBN 978-1-5362-1912-8 (hardcover)
ISBN 978-1-5362-2953-0 (paperback)

22 23 24 25 26 27 APS 10 9 8 7 6 5 4 3 2 1

Printed in Humen, Dongguan, China

This book was typeset in Amasis MT Pro.
The illustrations were created digitally.

MIT Kids Press
an imprint of Candlewick Press
99 Dover Street
Somerville, Massachusetts 02144

mitkidspress.com
candlewick.com

CONTENTS

INTRODUCTION

ON A BOAT that's cruising through white-capped waves off the coast of Washington State, a dog raises her nose to the sky, sniffing for a scent that could help save an entire endangered species.

On a rocky slope in California, a herd of hungry goats fights the effects of climate change one leafy bite at a time.

In a garden in Detroit, a honeybee homes in on a flower, using her electrical sensing abilities to make the city greener.

Animals have extraordinary senses, refined by evolution over millions and millions of years. Their unique biologies give many animals keener vision, hearing, taste, touch, or smell than we have. Some animals can even detect types of energy that we can't sense at all, such as tiny electrical charges in the air or magnetic fields that surround the Earth.

While these skills help animals navigate through their own environments, humans have recognized their value for centuries. In this book, you'll meet eight different animals whose incredible super senses are helping people to address problems we all face, including global warming, pollution, and world-wide pandemics.

You'll dive with a bomb-detecting dolphin, fly alongside a photo-delivery pigeon, and sail the high seas with a poop-sniffing dog detective on a mission to save endangered killer whales. You'll learn a honeybee's electric secrets and get an insider's look into what might be the biggest animal experiment of all time—so big that part of it happens in outer space.

Along the way, you'll learn about the biology and brain science behind these super senses, as well as the research and technologies they've inspired. You'll also explore the ethical issues that arise when humans team up with animals. And you'll try some activities that will show you what it might be like to have some of these super senses yourself.

Are you ready to jump in? Let's take a look at what people and other animals can do when we put our heads together . . . plus our noses, antennae, gills, and whiskers.

CHAPTER 1
DETECTOR DOGS

TO SAVE ENDANGERED SPECIES, SOME DOGS FOLLOW THEIR NOSES.

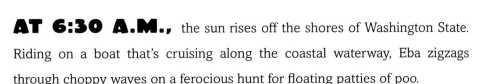

AT 6:30 A.M., the sun rises off the shores of Washington State. Riding on a boat that's cruising along the coastal waterway, Eba zigzags through choppy waves on a ferocious hunt for floating patties of poo.

Eba is a snuggly brown-and-white terrier mix and possibly the only dog in the world trained to sniff killer whale poop. From May through October, when an endangered population of killer whales known as the Southern Residents migrates through, Eba and Dr. Deborah Giles, the human scientist she works with, stay ready. When they get a call that killer whales, also called orcas, have been spotted in the area, they hop on their boat and head to the spot where the whales were sighted.

As they get close, Giles (she goes by her last name) slows down the boat, and they steadily crisscross through the waves, searching for sticky blobs of poop that bob on the surface and smell like sour old fish. These poop blobs may be red, green, brown, or yellow, and Eba can smell them as far as twenty football fields away. When she gets a whiff, she starts whining, licking her lips anxiously, and moving in the direction of the scent so Giles knows where to guide the boat. If they're lucky, they'll find thick, gooey, cake batter–like whale poop floating on the surface. When they do, Giles scoops it up using a big beaker attached to a long pole and brings it back to shore.

EBA USES HER SUPER-SENSITIVE NOSE TO FIND KILLER WHALES.

Dr. Giles is a killer whale biologist. She and Eba are both members of Dr. Samuel Wasser's lab at the University of Washington's Center for Conservation Biology. Southern Resident killer whales are the only

endangered killer whales in the United States, and scientists want to find the best way to protect them. Since 2005, Giles has been patrolling the waters off the Pacific Northwest to understand why there are fewer whales coming through and whether the ones that do pass by are healthy. Since it's hard to run tests on whales as they're swimming through the ocean, scientists like Wasser and Giles act like detectives and look for things the whales leave behind that can offer clues about what they're eating and what kinds of dangers they're encountering.

A big, sticky blob of whale poop can tell scientists all kinds of things: what species of fish the whales are eating, if the whales are having babies, and if they're feeling stressed out. (Just like people, whales make special hormones

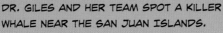
DR. GILES AND HER TEAM SPOT A KILLER WHALE NEAR THE SAN JUAN ISLANDS.

when they feel scared or uncomfortable, and those hormones come out the same way that digested food does.)

But finding clues like whale poop is a huge challenge. The poop floats on the surface for only a short time—thirty minutes or less—before sinking or being consumed by small, poop-eating sea creatures, which is why Eba and her super-sensitive snout are so important to this work.

KNOW YOUR NOSES

Humans can also smell whale poop, but they have to be much closer to the source. So how does Eba find it from so far off?

Most scientists believe that dogs have two major biological advantages compared to people when it comes to detecting smell. The first is a super-sensitive nose that can pick up incredibly small traces of odor. When Eba sniffs something in the air, special cells located deep in the back of her nose—starting about where the top of her nose meets the bottom of her eye sockets—detect the scent and send signals to alert her brain. These cells are called **OLFACTORY RECEPTORS**.

Humans have olfactory receptors, too. You have about six million of them in your nose, which is why you can recognize a huge range of different odors—anything from freshly baked cookies to dusty old books to the way it smells outside after it rains. But scientists estimate that dogs have about 300 million olfactory receptors.

OLFACTORY RECEPTORS: special cells that enable living things to detect scents

Plus, Eba's body maximizes every single one of those receptors. When a human breathes, the air quickly passes by the olfactory receptors and heads straight to the lungs. When dogs breathe, most air goes

OLFACTORY EPITHELIUM: *a spongy tissue inside the nasal cavity that's covered in mucus and contains cells that detect odors*

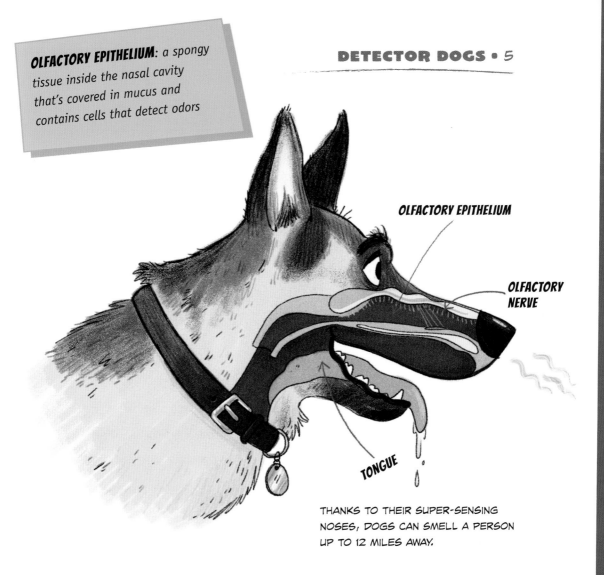

OLFACTORY EPITHELIUM

OLFACTORY NERVE

TONGUE

THANKS TO THEIR SUPER-SENSING NOSES, DOGS CAN SMELL A PERSON UP TO 12 MILES AWAY.

to their lungs, but a flap of tissue deep in their nose diverts a small amount of air—about 12 percent—just for smelling. This small bit of air smacks directly into a slimy organ called the **OLFACTORY EPITHELIUM**, which is basically a labyrinth of spongy tissue and curvy bones, all covered in snot.

If a tight, complicated maze dripping with snot sounds tough to get through, that's exactly the point. As air works its way through the olfactory epithelium, odor molecules get trapped in the sticky nooks and crevices.

SNOUTS BUILT TO SNIFF

Dog noses are cute—but they're also booger-resistant marvels of engineering. Have you ever noticed those slits on the sides of a dog's nostrils that look like curlicues? Like humans, dogs breathe in through their nostrils, but unlike us, they breathe out through these tiny slits. The small openings push exhaled breath away from the dog's face to prevent it from mixing with incoming air and diluting odors.

Even boogers don't get in the way of smelling. Snot in the back of our noses catches dirt and germs we breathe in throughout the day. Our nose hair pushes this dirt-covered snot away from our lungs and to the front of the nose, where it dries and sticks until we grab a tissue. Humans get boogers as a normal part of daily life, but dogs don't have nose hairs like we do—when their snot traps dirt, it goes the other way, to their stomach. Unless there's an unusual situation, like they happen to inhale

a hunk of dirt or have allergies or an infection that would cause extra nasal discharge, dogs don't get boogers.

WHEN DOGS EXHALE, THE CURLICUE-LIKE SLITS ON THE SIDES OF THEIR NOSES PUSH OUTGOING AIR AWAY FROM THEIR FACES, ENABLING THEM TO SMELL THE INCOMING AIR MORE CLEARLY.

Millions of olfactory receptors pounce and analyze the molecules' different shapes, sizes, and chemical compositions. Then they send that information to the other major organ that allows dogs to smell somewhere between ten thousand and one hundred thousand times better than people: their phenomenally odor-focused brain. While the nose detects odors, the brain determines what the odor is: clean laundry, a crackling fire, or moldy cheese. Dogs have smaller brains than we do, but the part that's used for recognizing smells is huge by comparison—about forty times bigger than ours.

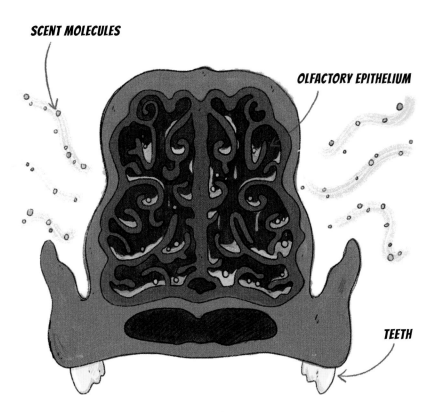

ODOR MOLECULES GET TRAPPED IN THE STICKY, MAZE-LIKE OLFACTORY EPITHELIUM.

Working together, this bigger smell-recognizing brain area, the complicated system of trapping odor molecules, and the overwhelming number of olfactory receptors make dogs like Eba phenomenal at their scent-sniffing jobs—and able to make unique contributions in the fight to save endangered species from extinction.

INVESTIGATING ORCAS

As whales swim in groups called pods, they leave behind clues about what they have been eating and encountering. Most of the clues look pretty

SMELL-OFF! HUMAN VERSUS DOG

If odor detection were an inter-species Olympic event, dogs would beat humans every time . . . almost. Dogs can detect a much wider range of scents than people can, but there are a few odors that humans can sniff out just as well as dogs. In fact, you might have one in your own kitchen: people are as good at detecting the smell of bananas as dogs are.

Why? Some scientists believe that the reason goes all the way back to the first humans. Early humans lived on food they hunted or gathered, so finding fruit was an important part of life for us. Canines don't need fruit as part of their diets, so detecting that smell wasn't as important to them. As both species evolved, humans got better at using our less sophisticated noses to find fruit while dogs used their more sensitive snouts to track other things, like hair, sweat, blood, and other scents associated with prey. Thousands of years later, dogs are clearly the superior sniffers overall, but when it comes to smelling bananas, it's anyone's game.

disgusting to everyone except for scientists, who know how valuable they are. For instance, when some species of whales die, they leave thick sticks of earwax longer than a large dinner fork. These sticks are made of a substance called **KERATIN**. When whales are eating regular meals, they produce light-colored layers of keratin; when they're migrating and aren't eating regularly, they produce dark-colored layers.

Slice open one of these earwax sticks and, similar to the rings in a tree stump, the light and dark layers tell a story about how long the whale lived, when it ate (and didn't), and what kinds of toxins or pesticides it may have encountered.

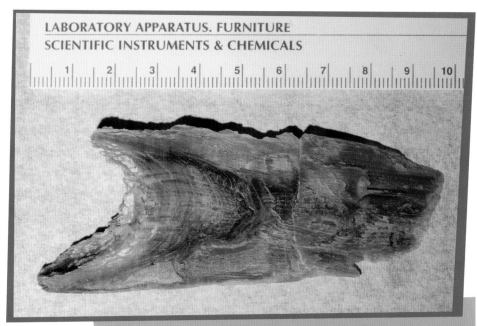

LIGHT AND DARK KERATIN BANDS IN WHALE EARWAX CAN HELP SCIENTISTS DETERMINE HOW OLD THE WHALE WAS.

Whales also leave things behind when they're alive. Whales pee as they're swimming and shed bits of skin and hair. (You may not think of whales as hairy, but the fist-size bumps on the backs, heads, or fins of some whales are actually really big **HAIR FOLLICLES**.)

THE BIG BUMPS YOU SEE ON THE HEADS AND FINS OF HUMPBACK WHALES LIKE THIS ONE ARE ACTUALLY HAIR FOLLICLES.

The problem is that these samples are usually tiny, and ocean currents often just wash them away. The largest and most reliable thing whales regularly produce is poop.

Whales poop out liquidy clouds of feces so big that divers have nicknamed them "poo-nadoes." Smaller particles dissipate in the ocean, but other parts of these poop clouds rise to the surface as blobs that could be as small as a single bean or as big as a large dinner plate. "Those are the fantastic samples," Giles says, adding that bigger poop samples offer scientists more information about the whales and generally are a sign that the whales are doing well. "I dream of poop like that."

Once Giles and her team scoop up one of these poop blobs, she puts the sample in a machine that spins fast enough to separate the poop from the ocean water it's in. Then she sends the solid bit off to Dr. Wasser's lab, where the sample gets analyzed to understand what kinds of food waste, hormones, toxins, and microscopic critters are inside it.

Right now, Eba's job is more important than ever. Southern Resident

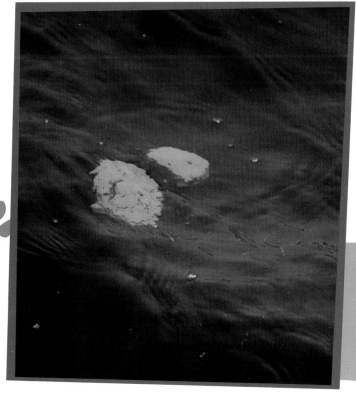

BLUE WHALES USUALLY PRODUCE ORANGEY-RED POOP, LIKE THE STUFF SEEN HERE, BUT WHALE POOP CAN ALSO BE BROWN, GREEN, OR YELLOW.

whales are among the most critically endangered marine mammals in the world. Compared to years ago, Giles sees fewer whales coming through, and the ones that are migrating outside of Washington State leave evidence indicating that they're struggling. She says that ten years ago, her team could easily find gummy patties of poo the size of buoyant pancakes. Now she's lucky to find diluted bits the size of your pinky finger.

That shrinking poop size is a sign that the whales aren't eating enough to have big poops; in fact, they are starving. Warming waters, disease, pollution, poor fisheries

"I DREAM OF POOP LIKE THAT."

management, and ecosystem destruction are killing off Chinook salmon and other fish the whales eat. There's also research showing that loud noises from shipping vessels and underwater construction can drown out the sound pings whales use to find food and mates.

As Southern Resident whales struggle to survive, every single poop sample captured is vital to figuring out how to help the whales recover. Eba, and other dogs who are trained to do conservation work, are ready for the challenge. After locating a poop sample, Eba gets a snuggle and time to play with her toys. But it won't be long before she's back on the job, pushing science forward one sniff at a time.

EBA LOVES TO PLAY BETWEEN POOP-SNIFFING SESSIONS.

DETECTOR DOGS AROUND THE WORLD

Whales aren't the only creatures detector dogs protect. Around the world, keen-nosed dogs trained to follow specific scents vigilantly work to keep animals and people safe.

On the Japanese island of Amami-Oshima, for example, dogs protect native birds, frogs, and rabbits from the small Indian mongoose, an invasive species that looks like a weasel and has few natural predators in the area. Detector dogs, trained on the animal's scent, help find hidden mongoose burrows so humans can thin their numbers.

In Mombasa, Kenya, a port where illegal animal products like ivory often enter the country, detector dogs protect endangered elephants and rhinos by helping to shut down wildlife trafficking. Thousands of shipping containers come through the port each day, and in just a few whiffs, these dogs know if there's ivory inside that needs to be seized.

In the small village of Great Horwood, in England, an organization called Medical Detection Dogs teaches pups how to sniff out disease. Trained to pick up on faint traces of odors that humans give off when we have certain diseases or infections, these dogs learn to detect conditions like malaria, diabetes, and some kinds of cancers and neurological conditions. Some go to live with patients and are trained to alert their owners if they smell certain odors that might precede an emergency such as a diabetic attack. Others participate in studies sniffing human samples and helping scientists develop robotic noses that can detect diseases just as well as detector dogs can.

BIO-DETECTION DOGS CAN BE TRAINED TO SNIFF MANY DIFFERENT DISEASES, INCLUDING COVID-19.

ACTIVITY
FOLLOW YOUR NOSE

How well can you follow a scent trail?

TO FIND OUT, YOU'LL NEED:

- a partner
- a dry, open outdoor area you can easily walk through
- a piece of cloth, such as a bandana, kitchen rag, or old T-shirt
- a nontoxic liquid with a strong smell, such as perfume, lemon juice, or vinegar (and permission from an adult to use it)

1. Start with your partner standing far enough away so they won't be able to hear your footsteps, and have them close their eyes.

2. While their eyes are shut, pick a place where you would like your scent trail to start and drop the cloth there.

3. Take two steps in any direction you choose, and place a drop or two of the smelly liquid on the ground. Repeat up to ten times, taking note of where you're moving.

4. When you're done laying the scent trail, go back to the dropped cloth and tell your partner to open their eyes and join you there.

5. Let your partner sniff a little of the smelly liquid you're holding, then see if they can follow the trail you made. (They'll probably need to get close to the ground.)

6. When they're done, it's time to switch roles!

BONUS If you and your partner are able to find the scent trails pretty easily, then try adding more turns to the trail or using more subtle scents. If you found it pretty difficult, try it with a stronger scent or in a new outdoor space, and don't give up! Studies show that people who are learning to track scents get better with practice.

CHAPTER 2
FAST FERRETS

THE PIPES ARE CURVED and black on the inside—so dark, it's hard to see if an end exists at all. They sit deep down in the earth, buried under layer after layer of dirt, at a depth about equal to the height of a full-grown man. They're narrow and cramped, musty and dank, and for a ferret wearing a tiny backpack, they're the perfect place to work.

In England, a snow-white, pink-nosed ferret named Cynthia happily scampers through these underground pipes. Her small, bendy body is ideal for moving through narrow spaces. Cynthia and the fifty other ferrets she lives with help humans with two tasks—running cables through skinny underground pipes and replacing pipes when they break. To dart through those long narrow spaces, these ferrets use a tool that happens to grow right on their faces: whiskers.

FERRETS' WHISKERS HELP THEM DETERMINE IF THEIR BENDY BODIES CAN FIT INTO NARROW OPENINGS.

For humans to reach an underground pipe—some of which are longer than six Olympic-size swimming pools—they would need to dig up the entire length of the pipe. That means high costs, hours of labor, and tearing down anything sitting on the ground above the pipe, which could be an important historical building or land that's vital to preserve. Cynthia, however, only needs a way in and a way out to get to an underground pipe, and she can run through it without disturbing anything on the ground above.

That's why James McKay, a ferret trainer and **ZOOLOGIST**, has brought Cynthia and five other ferrets to a shopping mall in Leicester, England.

When shoppers park their cars at the mall, automated barriers go up and down to regulate traffic. At the right moment, bursts of air from flexible underground pipes push the barriers up, but one of these pipes has broken and the barriers can't move at the right time.

No one wants to dig up the parking lot to change out the pipe, so James has brought a team of ferrets with different attributes—some small, some brave, some particularly strong—to get the job done.

ZOOLOGIST: *a scientist who studies animals*

A FOUL-SMELLING BANDIT
BY ANY OTHER NAME

How did you get your name? You might be named in honor of a relative. Maybe your name comes from your family's culture or religion, or it might be rooted in another language or ancestry. Ferrets are named after one of their favorite hobbies: stealing small objects and taking them back to their burrows. The proper scientific name for a ferret is *Mustela putorius furo,* which literally translates to "stinky weasel-like little thief." Yikes! If you were named after your worst quality and your favorite hobby, what would your name be?

PIPE DREAMS

The broken parking lot pipe sits deep beneath the surface in an underground channel—a narrow space that's designed to hold lots of different pipes and cables in one central place. To give the ferrets access to the channel, the construction crew digs two holes: one where the broken pipe starts and one where it ends. Each hole is the depth of a full-size refrigerator. Since it's too deep for James to safely drop a ferret directly into this underground channel, these four-footed workers will take the elevator today.

James slips a ferret named Roger into a tiny green fluorescent vest and a small harness. The vest distinguishes Roger from other critters who may be hanging around the construction site. The harness has a very long, very strong cord attached to it, as well as a small device that sends radio signals. James places Roger on a small platform, then carefully lowers the platform down, down, down into the channel.

When this tiny elevator stops, Roger tries to move through the channel, but his whiskers bend. He's too big. He won't be able to run through. James brings Roger back up to the surface, then puts the vest and harness on a smaller ferret named Jenny. Jenny heads down the elevator and into the channel, but quickly turns around. Something—maybe a strange smell or sound—has frightened her, and she won't enter the channel again.

Finally, it's Cynthia's turn. James gets Cynthia suited up and lowers her. She takes off in a flash. Ferrets naturally love to burrow and explore new places, so Cynthia is thrilled to scurry through this secret underground space, pulling the cord with her into the thick darkness as she goes.

HAIRY HELPERS

VIBRISSAE: the scientific term for whiskers

Like detector dogs—and many other working animals—Cynthia has a keen nose, which is crucial for her job. But the sensory system in her whiskers also helps her navigate through tight, dark spaces. Whiskers allow animals to feel the shape, size, and texture of things around them, even when it's too dark to see.

Better known as **VIBRISSAE** to scientists, whiskers are made mostly of keratin—the same material that makes up your hair and whale earwax—and they look like thick, extra-long hairs.

But unlike the hair on your head, whiskers also have tiny pockets of blood and nerve fibers around the base of them. These nerves, called

WHEN THEY'RE NOT ON A JOB, JAMES MCKAY'S
FERRETS TRAIN BY RUNNING THROUGH TUBES.

MECHANORECEPTORS, basically transform whiskers into teeny-tiny feelers, which may be as sensitive as your own fingertips. Animals can use their whiskers to feel different objects and textures, and they can detect changes in the way that air or water moves around their whiskers, letting them know if something they can't see, smell, or hear is close by.

Not all whiskers are the same. They can be long or short, movable or immobile. Animals use their whiskers in different ways. Some casually brush

DO CATFISH HAVE WHISKERS?

Sort of. Catfish look like they have whiskers, but each of those long "hairs" on a catfish's face is actually an organ called a barbel. Barbels contain taste receptors, which are also found all along a catfish's body. As these fish swim through murky waters at the bottom of rivers or lakes, their barbels sweep the ground and surrounding water, tasting everything in hopes of finding dissolved particles that have fallen off of potential food sources, as well as traces of carbon dioxide that tiny edible fish exhale as they swim by. Because their taste receptors are on the outside, catfish basically lick an entire river to find food they can put in their mouths. Imagine how life would be if you tasted anything you touched!

their whiskers against nearby objects, while others flick their whiskers up to twenty times per second to help them sense their surroundings.

Nearly all mammals have whiskers—humans being one of only a few exceptions—and while we mostly picture whiskers growing out of the face, they sometimes grow on other parts of the body, too. For example, many animals, including felines from small house

SOME ANIMALS CAN MOVE THEIR WHISKERS ONLY BACK AND FORTH, BUT MICE CAN MOVE THEIRS IN ANY DIRECTION.

cats all the way up to great big tigers, have hairs on their front legs called **CARPAL WHISKERS**, which help them feel whether prey they've caught is still twitching or if it's really dead.

So how exactly do whiskers like Cynthia's work? Basically, like a map, says Dr. Robyn Grant, a biologist at Manchester Metropolitan University, in England. Facial whiskers usually grow in rows and columns, just like a grid. The number of whiskers varies by species—rats, for example, have up to seventy facial whiskers, whereas manatees have roughly two thousand on their faces and about 3,300 more across their entire bodies. But no matter the number, all whiskers function basically the same way: mechanoreceptor nerve fibers detect a change in the environment and relay the precise type and location of that change to the brain.

CARPAL WHISKERS: specialized hairs found just above the paws on many animals. Animals use carpal whiskers to gather information about things they're holding in their paws, including prey.

IN COLD WATERS, SEALS' WHISKERS STAY WARM THANKS TO A SPECIAL SUPPLY OF BLOOD IN THEIR NOSE AND MOUTH AREAS.

Exactly how much information those nerve fibers pick up varies from species to species. Some animals have lots of mechanoreceptors, making their whiskers very sensitive. Seals, for example, have ten times more nerve fibers around their whiskers than rats do, and they use them when hunting. When a tasty fish swims by, seals use their super-sensing whiskers to pick up on the ripply trail left behind and to track that fish from up to half a football field away.

In dark places, whiskers are a big biological advantage, Robyn adds. Animals with the longest and most sensitive whiskers usually live in dark environments, either underwater or on land, and their whiskers help them navigate dark spaces. Without much light underground, Cynthia uses her whiskers, along with her other senses, to figure out if the channel holding a pipe is big enough for her to fit through, as well as if there are dangerous objects or obstacles along the way.

Whiskers are also teaching scientists a lot about how animals sense and navigate the world, and that knowledge benefits humans in a lot of different ways. Robyn, for example, studies animal whiskers in order to design artificial robo-whiskers that can help robots maneuver through dark spaces using touch. One day, these machines may be able to explore places that real

DR. ROBYN GRANT'S TEAM DESIGNS MACHINES LIKE THIS ONE TO EXPLORE HOW ROBOTS MIGHT USE WHISKER-LIKE APPENDAGES TO NAVIGATE DARK AND DANGEROUS PLACES.

whiskered animals like Cynthia can't venture into, such as the deep ocean, outer space, or even inside the organs and vessels in our bodies.

FOLLOW THAT FERRET

Back at the shopping mall, Cynthia is rushing through the underground channel. Up on the surface, James McKay also has a job. The tracker on Cynthia's backpack is sending radio signals to a corresponding device James holds in his hand. As Cynthia scampers underground, James runs along with her on the surface, following her every move. He will meet her at the end of the pipe if she makes it through or back at the beginning if she encounters something that forces her to stop and turn around.

WHAT WHISKERS TELL SCIENTISTS ABOUT YOUR BRAIN

Humans don't have whiskers, but scientists can learn a lot about people by looking at sensory systems we don't have. Whiskers are actually really important to **NEUROSCIENTISTS** because, in some animals, it's easy to see where touch signals are processed in the brain.

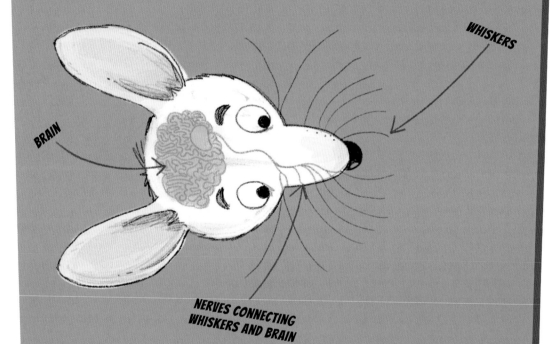

WHISKERS

BRAIN

NERVES CONNECTING WHISKERS AND BRAIN

EACH INDIVIDUAL RAT WHISKER CORRESPONDS TO A SPECIFIC SPOT IN THE RAT'S BRAIN. THIS SPECIFICITY HELPS SCIENTISTS BETTER UNDERSTAND HOW RATS' BRAINS PROCESS THE SENSE OF TOUCH.

NEUROSCIENTIST: a scientist who studies how our brains and nervous systems work

Unlike humans, some animals, including rats, mice, and gerbils, have a unique structure in their brains called the barrel cortex. This structure contains a grid that matches up exactly with the rows and columns of whiskers that these animals have on their faces. When a single whisker brushes against an object, sensory signals move from nerve fibers in that whisker follicle to the corresponding spot on the barrel cortex grid, allowing scientists to trace the exact path signals take from the whisker to the brain and to study what happens if that path gets disrupted. Humans don't have a barrel cortex, and it's much less clear which specific cells in your brain help decide if you're touching a fluffy kitten or an ice cube.

For researchers, this ability to see the exact brain cells that are activated when whiskers touch something is like a key that unlocks all sorts of cool scientific discoveries on brain cell and circuit organization. Researchers know, for example, that if you cut a single whisker a few days after a rat is born and keep cutting it as the whisker regrows, the rat's brain changes and adapts. The barrel cortex, which starts developing shortly after birth, reorganizes itself to compensate for the lost whisker, and that actually has a lot of implications for people. This kind of brain rewiring and adaptation is called **NEUROPLASTICITY**, and it happens in our brains, too. When people have a brain injury or if they undergo surgery in which part of their brain is removed, some are able to relearn things they lost, like the ability to walk or talk, even if the parts of their brain that used to be responsible for those functions never fully heal.

Studying how whisker systems work and how animal brains compensate when those systems are damaged can offer clues about how our own brains learn to recognize what we touch, inspire new methods for helping the brain adapt after injury, and guide how touch-sensing devices, such as prosthetic limbs that allow users to feel movement and textures, are designed.

NEUROPLASTICITY: the brain's ability to change and reorganize its cells and networks

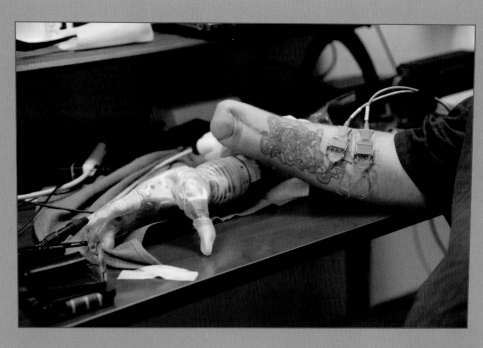

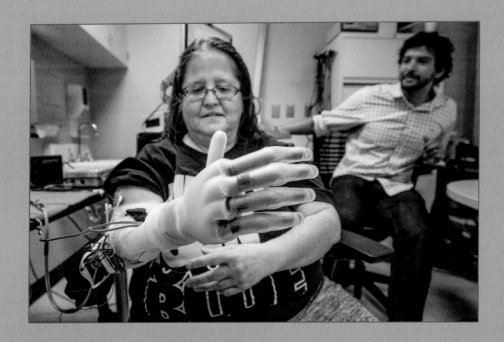

SCIENTIFIC STUDY OF HOW THE SENSE OF TOUCH WORKS HELPS ENGINEERS DESIGN MIND-CONTROLLED PROSTHETICS LIKE THIS ONE AT THE UNIVERSITY OF MICHIGAN. ONE GOAL IS FOR PROSTHETICS OF THE FUTURE TO ENABLE THEIR WEARERS TO SENSE TEMPERATURES AND TEXTURES.

Cynthia makes it all the way through to the end, where James is waiting with an elevator ride to the surface and plenty of her favorite treat—liver paste. "My ferrets would trade their granny for a lick of the liver paste," James says.

Cynthia's task is done, and now the human construction workers step in. The crew takes the cord that Cynthia pulled through the channel and ties a new flexible, rubbery pipe to it. They gently bend the new pipe, feed it into the underground channel, and use the cord to slowly thread it through. Once it's in place, they detach the old pipe and solder the new one in. In no time, the pipe is pumping air and the traffic control system is back up and running.

JAMES MCKAY'S WORKING FERRETS WEAR TINY TRACKING DEVICES THAT ALLOW HIM TO FOLLOW THEIR MOVEMENTS UNDERGROUND.

"MY FERRETS WOULD TRADE THEIR GRANNY FOR A LICK OF THE LIVER PASTE."

James brings Cynthia, Roger, and Jenny home. The ferrets will spend their days playing and training by running through the practice tubes James has set up in his yard—until they're called for their next underground adventure.

THE FERRET AND THE BEGINNING OF THE UNIVERSE

Construction sites aren't the only places where ferrets have saved the day. In the 1970s, one particular ferret named Felicia held a job of galactic importance: she helped scientists better understand how our universe was born.

In Illinois at the National Accelerator Laboratory, now called FermiLab, scientists had spent four years building a particle accelerator—a machine that takes bits of matter that are too small to see and moves them at very high speeds. Incredibly strong magnets in the accelerator keep the particles close together and moving in the right direction.

You've probably heard of atoms—the teeny-tiny bits of matter that make up solids, liquids, and gases. The particles in the accelerator are even smaller, and when you smash them together at high speeds, weird things can happen. Sometimes they break, giving scientists insight about how they're constructed. Sometimes, just for an instant, they make new "exotic" materials unlike anything seen on Earth. (It would be a bit like if you smashed two oranges together and a new fruit unlike any you had ever seen before appeared, then suddenly vanished.)

On Earth, particles rarely move fast enough to create these types of high-energy, high-speed collisions. But

FELICIA THE FERRET HARD AT WORK

there was a time in history when collisions like these happened a lot: the moments right after the Big Bang, at the very beginning of our universe, when space was rapidly expanding and full of hot, dense bits of matter that frequently bumped into one another. That's why scientists believe that observing these high-energy collisions, and the exotic particles that sometimes come from them, can give valuable clues into what happened when our planet was born.

But making those observations requires a powerful particle accelerator, and in 1971, the National Accelerator Laboratory researchers just couldn't get theirs to work. The machine relied on more than one thousand giant magnets, each weighing as much as two adult elephants, to whip particles around a circular vacuum tube,

roughly the length of six hundred full-length school buses, until they were moving at nearly the speed of light. Every time researchers tried, the magnets failed. Scientists eventually realized that the culprit was actually just trash: tiny bits of metal left over from constructing the tube were throwing the magnets off.

The tube was narrow—about as wide as a tennis ball—and it needed to be cleaned out. So the scientists turned to ferrets. They adopted Felicia and dressed her in a collar with a string attached and a diaper to prevent ferret poop from disrupting the accelerator. Felicia refused to run through the main tube, so they moved her to a nearby testing lab that was under construction. There, they trained her to run, string in tow, through smaller sections of tube. When Felicia was on the other side, they attached the string to thick swabs and pulled them through to remove debris.

Felicia got fish heads and chicken treats as rewards. Researchers got clean equipment, and they figured out a Felicia-inspired solution to the trash problem in the main tube. Engineer Hans Kautzky designed an artificial "magnetic ferret," a rod with dust-attracting disks attached to it that could be pulled through the tube using a magnetic cord. The mechanical ferret got the job done, but it was never as efficient, or as loved, as Felicia.

ACTIVITY
TOUCH TEST

Ferrets have nerve fibers that are unevenly distributed all over their bodies. Some areas, like their whiskers, are very sensitive, while others are less so. The same is true for humans, and in this activity, you'll investigate just how sensitive your skin cells really are.

YOU'LL NEED:

- a partner
- a bandana or other blindfold
- five toothpicks
- a ruler

1. Blindfold your partner and have them hold out their hand, palm side down.

2. Hold two of the toothpicks very close together (but not touching each other) and gently touch them to your partner's skin. Without taking off the blindfold, ask your partner how many toothpicks they feel.

3. Now experiment with how far apart you hold the toothpicks, using a ruler to measure the distance between them. What's the shortest length where your partner can recognize that two separate objects are touching their skin? How close together can you bring the toothpicks before two objects touching the skin begins to feel like one?

4. Now switch and see how you measure up to your partner. What happens when you try this on other areas of your body, like your forehead, lips, feet, shoulder, back, belly, or elbows? The parts of your body where it's easiest to tell how many toothpicks are touching you are the ones that have higher concentrations of touch receptors. What happens when you add more toothpicks?

Activity used with the permission of Eric H. Chudler, PhD, Neuroscience for Kids

CHAPTER 3
SPECIAL DELIVERY PIGEONS

BETTY WAKES UP surrounded by a dozen other pigeons in her coop in Fort Collins, Colorado. She preens her white feathers and stretches out her brown-ringed neck before eating a nutritious, seed-filled breakfast. After she's flown a few warm-up laps around nearby Poudre Canyon, her handler suits her up with her bird-size backpack and brings her to the Cache la Poudre River for her first trip of the day.

Betty is a fine-feathered member of the Pigeon Express: a talented group of birds who, for the past twenty-five years, have been delivering photographs and messages for the whitewater rafting company Rocky Mountain Adventures. No matter how far down the river they're brought, Pigeon Express birds are able to travel straight back to their coop at rafting headquarters, and get there much faster than human delivery drivers can.

Betty and her friends are great at this job because they're homing pigeons—a variety of pigeon that's famous for being able to find its way home over very long distances, up to a thousand miles away. That's like being dropped off in Florida and making it all the way back to your apartment in New York, all without using any maps or apps.

Scientists think birds like Betty pull off their impressive long-distance trips using a few different senses. Keen seeing and smelling abilities enable pigeons to build mental maps of their environments over time, so they can always figure out where they are. Tracking the sun in the sky helps them orient themselves in terms of north, south, east, and west. And a mysterious other sense might allow them to tap into the Earth's **MAGNETIC FIELD**, a layer of magnetic attraction that surrounds the planet, which some animals can detect.

All these senses combine to give homing pigeons a knack for navigation—which is why they've been recruited as delivery birds for thousands of years, by everyone from ancient Olympic athletes to modern-day whitewater rafters.

PHOTO FINISH

The Pigeon Express first took off in 1995, before people had cell phones with digital cameras. Back then, most cameras used film, which had to be processed by a special machine or with chemicals in a darkroom.

The Rocky Mountain Adventures team wanted to send photographers to document rafters going through gnarly rapids or getting sprayed with big splashes. But they ran into a problem. By the time the photographer finished the trip, brought the film back to rafting headquarters, developed it, and printed the photos, the guests were impatient—or already long gone. The company needed a way to cut down the delivery time, so they looked to the sky.

MAGNETIC FIELD: the zone of attraction around any magnetic material, from a refrigerator magnet to the Earth's core

Homing pigeons are descended from rock doves, wild birds that live on cliffs in Asia, Europe, and North Africa. Humans have spent centuries identifying pigeons who were especially fast at getting home, and breeding them with other pigeons who were equally good or better. People then use these super-speedy pigeons as messengers, or sometimes race them against each other. Over time, this **SELECTIVE BREEDING** has made modern pigeons even more efficient than their ancestors.

To build a team of delivery birds, David Costlow, the original owner of Rocky Mountain Adventures, bought a small flock of homing pigeons from a nearby bird racer. He built a coop for them at the company headquarters in Fort Collins and trained the birds by bringing them farther and farther from their home coop, releasing them, and letting them find their way back. He even got them custom backpacks tailor-made to hold tiny film canisters.

PIGEON EXPRESS FLYERS TAKE OFF OUTSIDE ROCKY MOUNTAIN ADVENTURES.

HARDWORKING PIGEONS THROUGHOUT HISTORY

Using birds to make deliveries isn't exactly a new idea. Homing pigeons have helped humans for thousands of years. Here's how:

- **444 BCE:** An athlete named Taurosthenes brings a homing pigeon with him to the eighty-fourth Olympic Games in Athens, Greece. When he wins the wrestling competition, he sends news of his victory via his pigeon, who brings it to their home on the island of Aegina the very same day.

- **LATE 900s CE:** The ruler of North Africa, al-Aziz Billah, has a sweet spot for a particular kind of cherry from the city of Baalbek, Lebanon. So one day, his second-in-command arranges for a special delivery. Six hundred pigeons are sent from Baalbek to the palaces in Cairo. Every bird has a silk bag containing a single cherry tied to each leg. Al-Aziz and his guests have fresh cherries for dessert.

- **1167:** Sultan Nur ad-Din sets up a pigeon messaging network across the Middle East, so that all the large cities can communicate. Pigeon towers are built every fifty miles or so, with fleets of birds on hand in case there is any news.

- **1405:** A huge naval fleet of 317 ships sets sail from Suzhou, China. The ships communicate with drums, gongs, lanterns—and pigeons, which bring the more complicated messages across the water.

- **1849:** Paul Reuter, who will go on to found the Reuters news agency, opens an office in Aachen, Germany. He employs a flock of pigeons to bring stock prices and other urgent news between Paris and Berlin.

- **1870:** During the Franco-Prussian War, Prussia cuts Paris off from the rest of France, blocking roads and severing telegraph lines. To communicate, Parisians send gas balloons—which are like hot-air balloons—stocked with messages and pigeons out to other towns. The pigeons fly the replies, which are typed in tiny print, back to Paris.

- **1897:** The people of New Zealand's Great Barrier Island start a pigeon-based postal service to communicate with the mainland, which is ninety miles away. Soon there are two competing pigeon-gram services, each with its own special stamps—widely considered the first "air mail" stamps ever made.

DURING WORLD WAR I, US ARMY PIGEONS LIKE THIS ONE HAD ID NUMBERS STAMPED ONTO THEIR WINGS.

- **1918:** Pigeons aid American troops regularly during World War I, delivering messages to and from the trenches. One, named Cher Ami, helps to rescue a trapped group of soldiers—who are being accidentally shot at by their own side—by bringing a missive about their position to the commanders right in the nick of time. She is wounded in battle and receives a wooden leg, along with military honors.

- **2016:** Artist Duke Riley trains two thousand pigeons to fly in swoops and dips above Brooklyn wearing LED bands. All spring, they perform light shows on weekend evenings.

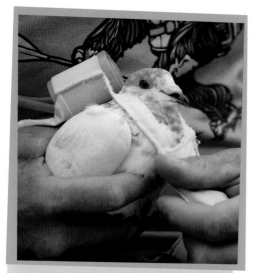

PIGEON EXPRESS BIRDS CARRY THEIR CARGO IN SPECIALLY DESIGNED BACKPACKS.

By the summer of 1996, the pigeons were pros at ferrying film. Before each rafting trip, a photographer would pick a favorite pigeon and put him or her in a special cage. As the rafters braved dips, sprays, and foaming rapids, the photographer and pigeon followed them from the shore.

When the photographer was finished snapping photos, they would put the roll of film into the pigeon's backpack and open the door of the cage. The pigeon would fly straight back to the coop at headquarters, where someone was waiting to receive the film and develop it. By the time the rafters got back to headquarters, their pictures were ready.

AN INNER COMPASS

Researchers have spent decades trying to figure out exactly how birds like Betty find their way home. Most agree that every homing pigeon has two important **WAYFINDING** tools, says Dr. Dora Biro, a scientist at the University of Oxford, in England, who specializes in bird navigation.

WAYFINDING: *the process of figuring out where you are in the world and how to get where you need to go*

One is a mental map, which tells Betty where she is in relation to where her coop is. The second is a compass sense, which allows her to identify geographical directions—what we call north, south, east, and west—so that she can get back home.

Let's talk about the compass first. On clear days, Betty gets her sense of direction from the position of the sun. Because the sun moves across the sky in an arc each day, rising in the east in the morning and setting in the west in the evening, it's always in about the same place at the same time. By cross-referencing the sun's location with her own internal clock, Betty and other pigeons can figure out which way is east and which way is west.

But that strategy won't work if it's cloudy. In that case, Betty may tap into a different source of information: Earth's magnetic fields.

Due to iron and other metals inside its core, the Earth is basically one giant magnet, with one magnetic pole located in the Arctic and the other in Antarctica. The rest of the planet is crisscrossed by zones of magnetic attraction called magnetic fields, which draw other magnetic materials to the north or south.

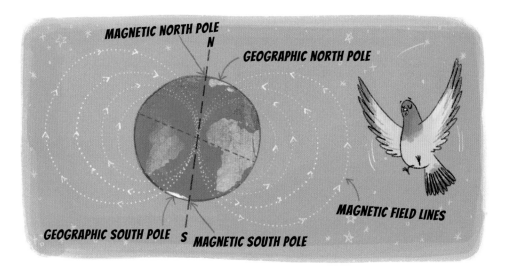

THE EARTH'S MAGNETIC FIELDS MAY HELP PIGEONS NAVIGATE.

At the Earth's surface, these magnetic fields are pretty weak—only about 1 percent as strong as a refrigerator magnet. But Betty can still detect them, and scientists aren't quite sure how. Her magnetic sense might come from minerals in her beak, special proteins in her eyes, or even an organ we haven't yet discovered. No matter how she does it, these fields help her figure out which way is north. Once she knows that, she can get on the right path.

THE MENTAL MAP

Now that Betty has checked her inner compass, she knows how to head in any direction. To decide which way to go, she calls on the other part of her navigational tool kit: her mental map.

Some scientists think Betty's map is also based on magnetic sensing: that she can place herself in space by detecting information about the magnetic field, almost as though she were reading coordinates on a map. Since she knows the magnetic coordinates of her home, too, she can point herself in the right direction and get back there.

Others think the mental map is based on smell. According to this theory, pigeons pay close attention to scents carried on air currents and use them to figure out their surroundings. For instance, maybe Betty was hanging out at

A NECESSARY SHIELD

Earth's magnetic field is useful for more than navigation. It actually extends past the planet's surface and into space, where it's called the magnetosphere. The magnetosphere is constantly repelling radioactive particles from the sun. Without it, those particles would bombard Earth, and make our planet totally unfit for life as we know it.

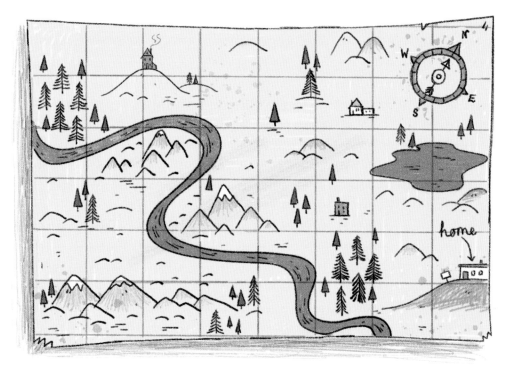

HOMING PIGEONS TURN SENSORY CUES INTO DETAILED MENTAL MAPS.

the coop one day and sniffed a whiff of fresh water brought in by an easterly breeze. When she ended up at the river, she recognized that she was at the source of that smell, realized she was east of home, and headed west.

Scientists don't know precisely how birds make their mental maps, but they do know that these maps are effective. Just like her predecessors, Betty prepared for her job as a young pigeon: her trainers brought her a little farther from the coop each day and let her fly back, allowing her to build up her map.

After just a few full trips from the rafting route back to her coop, Betty knew the way. Now she relies mostly on visual landmarks to get back, says Dora—something like *west at the river fork, then north at the gnarled tree, then home sweet home.*

EXPERIMENTS ARE FOR THE BIRDS!

Determined researchers have been trying to unlock the secrets of pigeons' super navigational sense for decades, and they've come up with some pretty wacky experiments to test their ideas. Some of the weirdest ones have led to the biggest breakthroughs.

By the 1950s, researchers had guessed that pigeons were using the sun as a compass. To test that theory, they gave some birds jet lag. They kept a flock indoors and used the indoor lighting to confuse their natural sense of time, shifting it six hours ahead of schedule. When the pigeons were allowed outside again, they thought it was morning when it was really afternoon and started heading in the wrong direction, demonstrating that they likely do use the sun as a clue.

In the late 1970s, researchers wondered if pigeons rely on sight alone to navigate. To find out, they put contact lenses on them that were designed to block their vision. The birds could see a little bit, but they couldn't make out the details required to recognize landmarks. When they still made it back to the loft, researchers knew that even if pigeons do use their vision when they can, other senses must also be at play.

Dr. Biro's work focuses on how pigeons navigate in familiar territory. She puts GPS trackers on her study subjects so she can see exactly how they make their way home. She theorized that if the birds were always navigating exclusively by the sun or magnetic fields, they would probably fly in as straight a line as they could. Instead, she has found that once pigeons figure out a route back from somewhere, they use it over and over again, even if it's not the most efficient. These findings suggest that visual landmarks do become important over time.

Hundreds of pigeon studies have taken place over the years. Each adds a new piece to the puzzle, and some contradict each other. It's up to researchers to pull all of this information together and figure out what's really going on inside these fascinating birds' brains.

SAME SKILLS, CHANGING NEEDS

No matter how she does it, Betty figures out where she is and where she needs to go. After a few quick circular swoops in the air, she flaps back home as fast as she can.

Homing pigeons can fly over seventy miles per hour, meaning they'd break the speed limit on most highways. While it takes about twenty minutes to drive from the end of the rafting route back to headquarters, Pigeon Express birds can make the trip in half the time, says David Terry, their manager.

These days, Pigeon Express birds are carrying things besides film. When photographers began using digital cameras, the pigeons started carrying memory chips instead. (Their backpacks were redesigned to hold them.) Now that photos can be emailed or texted instantly, the birds at Rocky Mountain Adventures are trained to fly with handwritten messages that rafters write to friends or relatives waiting back at headquarters—just as the birds' predecessors once did in ancient Greece. Generation after generation of a job well done.

THEY'D BREAK THE SPEED LIMIT ON MOST HIGHWAYS.

PIGEON EXPRESS BIRDS TRAVEL IN STYLE.

ANIMAL MAGNETISM

Pigeons aren't the only animals with a magnetic sense. Experiments have shown that lots of other species navigate that way, too. Blind mole rats use Earth's magnetic field to scurry through underground tunnels. Sea slugs reorient themselves with it after they're tumbled around by ocean currents. More recent research suggests that sea turtles may follow a magnetic path home to the beach where they were born in order to lay their eggs and that migratory birds and butterflies use information from magnetic fields to guide themselves south for the winter and north for the summer.

Scientists are still trying to figure out how this sense works in each of these animals. Do they have a special organ that helps them access these forces? Minerals or special proteins embedded in their eyes, ears, beaks, or antennae that respond to magnetic change? The answer may be different from species to species.

SEA SLUGS LIKE THIS NUDIBRANCH MAY USE A MAGNETIC
SENSE TO ORIENT THEMSELVES IN THE WATER.

In fact, so many different kinds of animals have a magnetic sense that some experts believe it originally evolved in a **COMMON ANCESTOR**, which would suggest that humans have it, too.

Some recent experiments by researchers in California have shown that our brains respond to changes in magnetic fields even though we're not aware of it. It's possible that as our other senses became dominant, we lost the ability to tap into this one.

GREEN SEA TURTLES NAVIGATE LONG DISTANCES,
LIKELY WITH THE HELP OF MAGNETIC FIELDS.

COMMON ANCESTOR: a single species from which at least two current species have evolved. For instance, experts think that all mammals besides marsupials, platypuses, and echidnas have a common ancestor that resembled a shrew.

ACTIVITY
MAPPING IT OUT

Just like a pigeon, you probably spend a lot of time traveling home from other locations. Pigeons find their way back to their coop by mentally mapping out their environment, keeping track of landmarks, directions, and even smells. Can you draw a multisensory map of your own homeward journey that would make a pigeon proud?

YOU'LL NEED:

- paper
- something to write or draw with

1. Think of someplace you and an adult regularly walk to and come home from—maybe school, your neighbor's house, or the corner store. You're going to map this trip. (You can also map a shorter trip, like from the kitchen to your bedroom.)

2. Draw your home or bedroom—your "home base"—in one corner of your map. Draw the other place—your neighbor's house, your school, the kitchen—in the opposite corner.

3. The next time you take this trip, pay attention to important landmarks—visual ones but also sounds, smells, and even textures. Does a dog usually bark when you walk by that house? Does that street corner always smell like roasted peanuts?

4. Fill out your map by drawing the most important landmarks. Which ones are helpful, and which might throw you off in the future? (For instance, does that roasted peanut cart move around a lot? You might not want to include it after all!)

5. Over time, like a pigeon, you can refine your map so that it's clear and constant.

Try giving your map to a relative or friend, and ask them to navigate to the same place. Go along with them. What do they notice that you missed, and vice versa?

Try this exercise with an even bigger area. If you were a pigeon, what sensory landmarks might you use to help navigate back home from the next town over? What about from the Statue of Liberty or the Golden Gate Bridge? Paper or digital maps can help you think this through.

CHAPTER 4

GOBBLING GOATS

IT'S A CLEAR SUMMER DAY in San Diego, and Rosita is ready for lunch. She trots a few steps up the hill where she's working today and eyes the dry brush all around. To humans, these plants are so dry that they're dangerous—a single spark could set the whole field ablaze. But to Rosita, they're a delicious meal.

Rosita is a brush abatement goat, one of roughly three thousand owned by the company Environmental Land Management Inc. She and her herd work in Southern California with their owner, Johnny Gonzales, and they have one job: to clamber over steep hills and rocky terrain, eating as many dried-out bushes, yellow grasses, and other crispy plants as they can. This dry brush is part of her natural diet. By removing it from steep and rocky places that are hard for people to access, Rosita and hundreds of other hungry hooved helpers prevent small fires from growing into out-of-control wildfires and create paths that help human firefighters put out flames. They do it all with their saliva, which neutralizes chemicals that make certain plants bitter and undesirable to other animals, and their mighty, microbe-filled digestive system.

SCORCHED EARTH

In California, a state that's hot and dry for most of the year and has huge stretches of wildland, fires happen frequently. Sometimes fires start because lightning or a fallen power line hits a patch of dry vegetation. Sometimes they're accidentally started by people who leave smoldering cigarette butts on the ground or don't fully put out their campfires.

Regardless of how they start, some wildfires can easily get out of control. Southern California gets a lot less rainfall than other places in the United States. Most of the rain that does come falls in winter and spring, keeping plants moist and less likely to catch on fire. But when it gets hot in the summer and dry and windy in the fall, these plants lose moisture and become more **FLAMMABLE**. One small spark, plus a little wind, is enough to burn an area the size of ten basketball courts in just five seconds.

A WILDFIRE IN IDAHO CONSUMES GRASSES IN FLAMES.

FLAMMABLE: *easily caught on fire or burned*

FIRE WHIRL!

In rare cases, fires can actually get so hot that they make their own weather systems. In extremely large wildfires, heat from the flames rises so quickly that it sucks in air surrounding the fire, pushing the flames upward. If the wildfire is super hot and it's windy, the flames can rise and swirl fast enough to become a tornado-like whirl of fire. Yikes!

A FIRE WHIRL BURNS AT THE GREAT DISMAL SWAMP NATIONAL WILDLIFE REFUGE.

Gusts of wind can spread the flames and fan the smoke high into the air, preventing firefighters in helicopters from dousing the blaze from above. With nothing to stop them, wildfires grow and grow and grow. They can burn down entire towns and drive some animals to the brink of extinction. In 2020, fires in California left an area twice the size of Rhode Island charred.

As global warming makes water scarcer, plants drier, and summers more sweltering, wildfires are getting bigger, hotter, and more frequent. In California, five out of six of the largest fires since the 1930s happened in 2020 alone.

FIREFIGHTERS DROPPING WATER ON A WILDFIRE BY HELICOPTER

Fires aren't always bad. In fact, many species of plants and insects need fire to survive. When fires burn off dry and dead plants, they create open space and send nutrients into the soil, where new plants can grow.

A CONSERVATION CONUNDRUM

One of the most surprising animals that benefits from fire is a tiny, fragile endangered butterfly called the Karner blue. Karner blue larvae eat only one thing: lupine plants, which grow on grass-covered prairie lands. If untended, prairie grasslands grow into shrublands, dense with plants that take the soil nutrients and sunlight that low-lying lupines need. Karner blues rely on wildfires to burn off shrubs and restore nutrients so new lupines can grow.

For scientists trying to save the butterflies from extinction, this creates big problems when deciding on the right conservation strategy. Should researchers set fire to butterfly habitat, killing some endangered larvae in the process? Or should they leave the land alone and risk shrubs killing the lupines and the butterflies, too?

As researchers battle over whether to use fire to boost butterfly numbers, some Karner blues are thriving in an unlikely spot: bomb testing grounds. At military weapons testing facilities, flying bullets and bombs often spark small fires on the grassy areas just outside of the impact zones. Many of the healthiest groups of Karner blues live just steps away from gunfire and explosions.

FIRE IS ESSENTIAL TO KARNER BLUE BUTTERFLIES' SURVIVAL.

But fires that burn out of control are dangerous. One way to prevent these wildfires from reaching homes is by thinning out the brush, especially in areas called **WILDLAND-URBAN INTERFACES** where human communities butt up against wildland. There are lots of different strategies for brush removal. Many Native American tribes, including the Yurok, Kumeyaay, and Karuk tribes of California, have long set small burns that eliminate overgrown brush before being put out. In the 1800s, when Native Americans were forcibly removed from their lands, these prescribed burns stopped. Soon after, government land managers started extinguishing small lightning-induced fires, too. Dead brush has piled up, so now, when there's a spark, wildfires can grow really fast. Many people are working to bring back Native American burning practices. Some land managers also cut down dead trees or have human workers trim brush to prevent fires. Others call on the goats.

BY EATING UP DEAD PLANTS AND BRUSH, GOATS HELP PREVENT FIRES FROM REACHING HOMES AND BUSINESSES.

FOUR·LEGGED FIRE PREVENTION

Rosita comes to work hungry. She's tan and brown, with white stripes streaking down her face, and while she doesn't look like an eating machine, she can swallow mouthfuls of weeds, tree limbs, brambles, and leaves. Goats can also eat plants like poison oak that irritate our skin.

GOATS CAN ALSO EAT PLANTS LIKE POISON OAK.

Rosita alone only eats a few pounds of plants a day. But when her eating talents are multiplied by a whole herd, areas that would take humans weeks to clear can be taken care of in just a few days. A herd of three hundred goats can clear one thousand to two thousand pounds of brush a day, and they can do it without using harmful chemicals, creating air pollution, or bringing in noisy machinery that human workers would need. They're cheaper, too: Johnny says that bringing in goats usually costs about half as much as having human workers clear large areas of land.

Rosita and her herd work all year round. Every day is different; the goats might be thinning out shrubs on the hills of a public park, devouring dry brush near buildings, or nibbling weeds on the slopes of a canyon. But they are always brought in with a plan. Johnny spends months working with local fire departments, land managers, and city planners to figure out which plants in particular areas are most flammable and how much the goats need to eat.

They target low-lying plants and weeds that can help a fire move along the ground, as well as taller plants like tangles of bramble and small trees. If these bigger plants ignite, fire can move upward, increasing its chance of burning communities or homes.

Once Johnny has a map of where exactly the goats need to eat, his team puts up a low-voltage electrical fence around the area. This fence has just enough zap to scare predators if they come too close but not enough to spark a fire. Then it's time to bring in the goats, anywhere from two hundred to six hundred for a job. Like children (and many adults if we're being honest), goats fill up on their favorite foods first, but Johnny has a strategy to make sure the goats eat the right plants. "You put enough goats together that if they don't eat what's in front of them, the other goats will," he explains. "There's a sense of competition."

Rosita and her herd can clear an area the size of sixteen tennis courts each day. They stay in the enclosure for a few days, munching on brush whenever they please, until the job is done. Goats aren't the only working animals on the scene. Johnny also brings in guard dogs to protect Rosita and her friends from predators like coyotes while they dine out.

HERDING DOGS KEEP THE GOATS SAFE BY PROTECTING THEM FROM PREDATORS.

GOATS VERSUS THE INVADERS

Goats can also help protect endangered plants. When making a fire safety plan, Johnny researches whether plants growing in that area are **NATIVE SPECIES** or **INVASIVE SPECIES**.

Native plants and animals are kept in check by predators that prevent them from multiplying out of control. But outside species might not have predators nearby. These invaders can quickly take over all the food and resources, killing native species and wrecking the entire natural food chain in the process.

Scientists estimate that in recent years, invasive species have played a major role in 25 percent of all plant extinctions, 33 percent of animal extinctions, and 70 percent of aquatic life extinctions. In the United States, roughly four out every ten plants and animals that are threatened or endangered are at risk because invasive species are making it hard to survive.

If Johnny knows where the invasive species are, he can place his goats in patches that are overgrown with these plants. The goats eat these invaders, and their digestive systems break down the seeds, preventing new sprouts from springing up after the goats have pooped. That's how goats help give native species a better chance of survival.

INVASIVE SPECIES: *a type of animal, plant, or microorganism that does not originally come from a specific region or ecosystem and can cause harm in its new environment*
NATIVE SPECIES: *a type of animal, plant, or microorganism that is originally from a specific region or ecosystem*

STRONG SPIT AND STOMACHS

Goats are **BROWSERS**, meaning they eat leaves, shoots, and twigs that grow on woody plants, and they're natural fire preventers because they have two body parts that are specially designed to demolish fire-prone vegetation. The first is the spit in their mouths.

Many plants contain chemicals called **TANNINS** that taste bitter, encouraging hungry insects to go somewhere else for their next meal. Some of the medicines we use and foods we eat, such as cranberries and coffee, contain low amounts of tannins. Unripened fruit has lots of these chemicals, which discourage animals from eating the fruit before the seeds inside it are fully developed—if you've ever bitten into an unripened apple or banana, you've tasted this for yourself—but as the fruit matures, tannin content drops and the taste gets sweeter.

The tougher parts of plants such as bark, leaves, wood, and stems are loaded with tannins, deterring many hungry animals from chowing down. But they don't bother goats! Goat saliva is brimming with special proteins that bind to tannins and neutralize them, transforming plants that taste bitter and gross to other animals into a tasty, edible meal.

The second body part that gives Rosita super fire-preventing powers is her stomach, which can effectively destroy tough vegetation. For goats, eating and digesting is an all-day affair. At mealtime, you carefully chew your food, swallow it, and move on with your day. Goats, and some other animals such as cows and sheep, basically swallow food whole, then spend hours spitting it back up, chewing it again, swallowing, and repeating. Eating, regurgitating, then re-eating the last meal you ate for hours sounds disgusting, but for goats, it works: this system is why they can digest all sorts of rough, woody, poisonous things we can't.

Just like in humans, when goats swallow food, it travels down the esophagus and hits the stomach, says Dr. Andrea Watson, an animal scientist at the University of Nebraska–Lincoln who studies nutrition in goats and similar animals. But while your stomach is basically a single sack made of muscle, a goat's stomach has four chambers that work together as one big digestion team. The first stop is the rumen, which contains a powerful soup made of bacteria and other microscopic organisms. This soup is dense—there are billions of microbes swimming around in a single tablespoon of rumen fluid, and

STOMACH THIS

Chewing already-swallowed food is far from the strangest way that animals digest. In a weirdest-digestion contest, lobsters would beat goats every time. A lobster's stomach is located in his head, just behind his eyes, and there's a big surprise inside: teeth. After food is swallowed, three teeth in the stomach called the gastric mill chew the food before it heads through the rest of the digestive tract and gets pooped out of the lobster's rectum, located just under his tail. Meanwhile, liquid waste is pushed into the bladder, which is just under the lobster's brain. It mixes with chemicals called **PHEROMONES** that animals use in communication, fighting, and finding mates. Then this mixture comes out of the base of the antennae. That's a long way of saying that lobsters pee from a gland under their eyes and when they do, they might just find a hot date.

PHEROMONES: special chemicals animals, including insects, produce that affect the behavior of other individuals of their species. Pheromones serve a variety of purposes, including communication, finding mates, marking trails or territory, and warning of a danger close by.

they're ready to break down a specific kind of fiber that holds bark, sticks, and plants together. But this bacterial soup can attack only pieces of food it can reach.

To ensure that every last bit of food gets smothered in microbes, the rumen joins forces with a smaller stomach chamber right next to it called the reticulum. They work together to basically treat the food like a hot potato that gets passed from the bacterial soup to the goat's mouth and back again. The bacterial soup attacks the outside layer, then the food gets brought back up to the mouth for more chewing, which breaks it down further and creates more spaces for bacteria to slide in, Andrea explains.

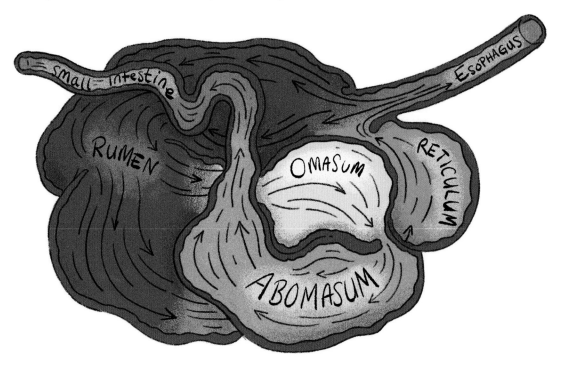

YOUR STOMACH IS ONE SINGLE ORGAN, BUT GOAT STOMACHS HAVE FOUR CHAMBERS WITH DIFFERENT FUNCTIONS, ENABLING THEM TO BREAK DOWN FOOD PEOPLE CAN'T EAT.

This chew-swallow-chew-swallow process goes on for hours. Over time, sticks and leaves are worn down into a liquidy sludge that moves into a small round organ underneath the rumen called the omasum. The omasum pulls water from the food sludge and sends it to other cells throughout the body, then pushes the food into a final chamber called the abomasum, which acts like your stomach. It contains special acids that break down many of the compounds that make up human food, such as proteins, fats, and carbohydrates. From there, the goat digestive tract looks a lot like your digestive tract. Remaining food goes through the small intestine, the large intestine, and the rectum, then exits the goat's body as poop.

READY TO CHOW DOWN

BORN FOR THIS

Unlike some other animals in this book, these goats don't need any special training to do their jobs. Brush and other flammable vegetation are already part of their natural diets, so all they really need to do to help people is show up in the right place, ready to eat.

Rosita's mighty mouth won't replace human firefighters—there are many brush abatement jobs that people can do better and more efficiently. But winning the war against wildfire requires many different strategies and tools, and goats are a good one. Rosita and her herd are happy to help. After a day of eating (and re-eating), they go home, get some sleep, and wake up ready to turn more dangerously dry land into a brushy breakfast.

ACTIVITY
FLAVOR FACE-OFF

Just like goats, humans use several different senses to choose our favorite foods—and taste might not factor in as much as you think.

Scientists believe that most of the sensory information we use to identify a specific flavor actually comes from our sense of smell and not our taste buds. When people lose their sense of smell, they often experience food completely differently.

This exercise is designed to help you determine what's doing the real tasting work—your nose or your mouth.

YOU'LL NEED:

- a partner
- a bandana or other blindfold
- three spoons
- three foods that have the same texture but different tastes. These could be three flavors of the same food, or they could be three different foods that have the same thickness and texture, like pudding, plain yogurt, and sour cream. You might want to try three different kinds of ice cream or flavors of jam, or three condiments, like ketchup, mustard, and barbecue sauce. (**IMPORTANT!** Ask your partner if they have any allergies or dietary restrictions.) Keep the foods out of smelling range: you and only you should know what foods you've chosen.

1. Have your partner sit somewhere comfortable, and blindfold them.

2. Have them hold their nose and open their mouth, then feed them a tiny taste of one of the foods. Without smelling it at all, can they tell what it is?

3. Now tell them to let go of their nose, and hold another taste of the same food under their nostrils.

4. Tell them to take a few deep breaths to smell the food, then taste it again. Do they notice any differences in taste?

5. Repeat for the other two foods. Can your partner tell what foods they're eating?

6. Now switch. Have your partner choose three new foods, then test your taste buds. Pay attention to how much smell, or lack thereof, alters how each food tastes, and what flavors you can detect first when you take smell out of the eating experience.

BONUS

Try adding a sweetener, such as sugar or maple syrup, or a spice, such as pepper or garlic powder, to your test foods.

CHAPTER 5
FIRST-ALERT FISH

LATE ON A WINTER EVENING, in a water treatment plant near Frederick, Maryland, a fish named Adrian rests calmly in his tank. Around him, seven of his coworkers do the same, in identical tanks of their own. They all breathe in and breathe out, their gills fluttering evenly. Nearby, a computer tracks their every move.

Adrian and his colleagues are young bluegills: shiny green-gray fish about the size of your hand, with big black eyes and a body shaped like a pumpkin seed. They work for a company called Blue Sources, and while they may appear laid-back, their gills are ever vigilant. By simply keeping still and breathing in their tanks, they are protecting the city's water supply, monitoring for contaminants that could make people sick.

KEEPING CLEAN

In most cities and suburbs, the water that flows through our faucets and taps comes from lakes, rivers, or reservoirs. (In rural areas, water also comes from groundwater wells.) It's piped from these natural sources to a **WATER TREATMENT PLANT**, where it goes through many steps to make sure it's safe to drink. As the water moves through the plant, big filters sift out dirt and clay, mixing machines spin away smaller particles, and workers add chlorine to get rid of some bacteria and microorganisms.

AT TREATMENT PLANTS, WATER GOES THROUGH A NUMBER OF STEPS TO MAKE IT CLEAN AND SAFE.

THE FIRST LINE OF DEFENSE

Rather than relying on first-alert fish to detect chemicals and other harmful materials in the water, it's better to keep the nasty stuff out of our streams and rivers in the first place. The Potomac Conservancy, a nonprofit dedicated to river health, releases "report cards" for the Potomac River—the largest river in the Frederick, Maryland, area, and the source of the Monocacy River, which supplies the water for the plant where Adrian works. In recent years, the Potomac has gotten mostly Bs and B minuses.

While some pollution in the Potomac comes from direct dumps and spills, most of it sneaks in more stealthily. As people construct buildings and pave roads and parking lots, rainwater that would have soaked deep into the ground is instead trapped at the surface. There, it picks up trash, gasoline, fertilizer, and other pollutants and rolls into the river, becoming **RUNOFF POLLUTION**. This often happens after big storms.

There are ways we can help. Volunteers with the Potomac Conservancy plant trees near rivers and along stream banks. These serve as natural filters, preventing pollutants from entering the rivers and streams. The volunteers also advocate for water protection laws that limit the use of harmful fertilizers, pesticides, and other chemicals. We can all help by properly disposing of trash and chemicals and by picking up litter we see lying around.

VOLUNTEERS HAVE HELPED THE MONOCACY RIVER GET CLEANER.

These actions work. Just fifteen years ago, the Potomac was getting Ds on its river report card. New laws, dedicated volunteers, and people's everyday choices have led to a huge improvement.

RUNOFF POLLUTION: *water that gathers pollutants and rolls into a river or stream rather than soaking back into the earth*

But sometimes there are other bad things in the water. Maybe a leaky boat spilled harmful chemicals into a river or a big rainstorm washed gasoline out of a parking lot and into a reservoir.

Testing for these contaminants is tough. There are special kits that can check for specific pollutants, but "there's no test to say whether water is toxic or not" overall, says David Trader, a US Army biologist who has spent years working on this problem.

But fish do those kinds of tests all the time. Because they need clean water to live, their bodies react strongly to anything that's not supposed to be there.

That's where Adrian and the other bluegills come in. Thanks to their extra-sensitive gills, they're great at detecting toxic chemicals, even in very low amounts. Scientists and engineers have designed a system that uses this super sense to alert human water quality technicians when something is amiss.

A COMPUTER THAT SPEAKS FISH

Some of the water for the city of Frederick comes from the Monocacy River, a twisty, sixty-mile waterway that flows out of the much larger Potomac. More than twenty thousand people use water from the Monocacy, and they rely on Adrian's water treatment plant and a few others to provide clean, safe water.

In the plant, water that has already been cleaned and treated flows through eight different tanks, each with its own fish on duty. The tanks are outfitted with electrical sensors that track how much the fish inside it is moving at any given time. All of a fish's muscle movements, from fin flicks to breaths, produce small amounts of electricity that these sensors can detect.

Normally, bluegills like Adrian breathe forty times per minute—about three times as fast as you do. And they don't move around very much.

A BLUE SOURCES FISH AT WORK. READOUTS FROM THE FISH'S
BREATHING HELP TECHNICIANS KNOW WHETHER THE WATER IS CLEAN.

HOW TO BREATHE UNDERWATER

Almost all animals need oxygen to live. Fish are no exception. They breathe in oxygen and breathe out carbon dioxide, just as we do. But instead of lungs, most fish use gills—super-efficient organs that are built to squeeze as much oxygen as possible out of the water.

When you take a deep breath, air flows into your lungs and fills up little sacs called alveoli, which are crisscrossed with tiny blood vessels. Oxygen enters the blood, swapping places with carbon dioxide. You exhale the carbon dioxide, and the oxygen travels through blood vessels around your whole body, where it helps to fuel your cells.

When Adrian or another fish takes a deep breath, the process is pretty similar. First, the fish opens his mouth and widens his **OPERCULA**—the flap-like covers that protect his gills. Water floods into his head and encounters the gills, which are filled with blood. Just like in human lungs, the oxygen enters the blood, which takes it all around the body. Meanwhile, the carbon dioxide gets left behind in the water, which the fish releases through his mouth.

But there's one big difference. The air we breathe is made up of about 21 percent oxygen. In water, that percentage is way, way lower. For every million molecules of water, there are only about ten molecules of oxygen that fish can use, which means gills have to soak up as much as they can.

A key way gills do this is through size. They might look small and compact, but they consist of folds and feathery branches that provide the gills with high surface area. (In one study, researchers measured the gills of a tiny mackerel and found that if they were unfolded, they would be about the size of a bandana.) It's as though the

OPERCULUM (PL. OPERCULA): the protective covering over a fish's gills that opens and closes in order for the fish to breathe

water has to pass through a complicated maze rather than just a short tunnel. The water is also in contact with the gills for a while, giving them time to pick up oxygen.

Gills existed long before lungs—in fact, scientists now think that the common ancestor of all vertebrates had gills. So next time you inhale, spare a thought for our fishy friends, who are working harder just to breathe easy.

A FISH GILL VIEWED AT 40X MAGNIFICATION, SHOWING ITS MAZE-LIKE PASSAGES.

THE FISH ARE "KIND OF LIKE COUCH POTATOES."

They were picked for this job in part because they're "kind of like couch potatoes," as David puts it.

If something is in the water that doesn't belong, Adrian will start breathing faster, opening and closing his mouth rapidly and quickly moving his opercula to fan the danger away. If that doesn't work, he'll start to cough.

Bluegills have two types of cough: a small, quick one, which experts have termed a high-frequency cough, and a larger, slower one, called a spike cough. Both types help them get rid of dirt, sand, chemicals, or anything else that could irritate their gills.

When he produces a high-frequency cough, Adrian puffs out his cheeks and then sucks them back in again. This pulls water through his mouth and over his gills more quickly than normal, as though he's clearing his throat: "Ahem!"

For a spike cough, Adrian quickly forces water out of his mouth, lowering the pressure inside his head. This makes the water rush back over his gills and out of his mouth, taking any obstructions or chemicals with it—almost like he's hocking up a loogie.

WRONG FOR THE JOB

The engineers who designed the water safety technology using fish as helpers auditioned many different species before choosing bluegills. Here are a few who didn't make the cut:

FATHEAD MINNOW: These minnows are common throughout North America. Scientists use them for other kinds of water-quality tests because they can tolerate harsher conditions than most fish. But they're too active to be happy hanging out in a water treatment tank all day.

LARGEMOUTH BASS: Bass really do have large mouths— some of them can open their mouths as wide as you can. They also have powerful coughs. But they grow fast, and a young bass might quickly get too big for his cubicle.

RAINBOW TROUT: Famous for their iridescent colors, rainbow trout are steady breathers, which works well with the computer monitoring system. But they can only live in cold water and aren't adaptable to different environments—making them unsuitable for a job that might require testing water in California, Maine, or anywhere in between.

As the sensors in Adrian's tank detect his movements, they send the information to a special computer. Most of the time, it's just his opercula moving slowly in and out—"steady as a rock," says David. The computer creates a readout graph that looks like a series of evenly spaced waves.

But if Adrian starts moving around, breathing faster or coughing, the readout changes. And if at least six of the eight bluegills in the system get jittery, it triggers an alarm. Human technicians then rush over and shut off the flow. They sample the water and run tests until they know what's wrong and how to fix it.

COMING TO A CITY NEAR YOU?

The US Army first started working with bluegills in the 1990s, as they were working to clean up a severely polluted area: a toxic waste site in Aberdeen, Maryland, where the military had once dumped explosives, cyanide, and other deadly chemicals. (One report of what was in the sludge was five pages long, in tiny type.) Although the dumping had happened many decades earlier, the chemicals still remained and were leaking into the Chesapeake Bay.

Over the years, containing the waste has required high-tech monitors, radar scanners, and even robots. As the last line of defense, the army recruited

KEEP OUT!

People also have ways of detecting and keeping out unusual stuff in the air. Do you cough when you accidentally burn toast to a crisp? That's your body's way of keeping smoke from getting into your lungs. Do your eyes tear up when your dad chops onions? They're trying to flush out an irritating—but harmless—chemical compound that onions release when cut.

bluegills. Any groundwater or rainwater that flows through the site gets cleaned at a treatment plant. Before it can leave the treatment plant and trickle into a nearby river, it has to pass the fish test to make sure it's not taking any harmful chemicals with it.

Bluegills have helped out at that toxic waste site for over thirty years now, and it's slowly getting cleaner. Since the 1990s, several other cities have put the fish to work for periods of time, including San Francisco, Cincinnati, and Washington, DC. Bluegills have successfully warned people about pollution in the Monocacy River, as well as in New York City's Kensico Reservoir.

Blue Sources, which bought the army's technology in 2014, is trying to put bluegills back into action in Washington, DC, and New York, where they

HUMAN WORKERS AT ABERDEEN PROVING GROUND, WHERE FISH ALSO HELPED CLEAN UP.

would complement the cities' other water testing programs. The company's motto? "Trust the Fish."

Blue Sources got Adrian from a fish hatchery. After his two-week shift, he gets some time off in a larger tank, where he eats, swims, and hangs out with other off-duty bluegills. When he grows too big to fit comfortably in his tiny tank, he'll be brought back to the hatchery where he was born, to live out the rest of his life in a pond with other bluegills.

A BLUEGILL FISH IN HIS NATURAL HABITAT

He's done his job. And the people of Frederick can brush their teeth without fear—all thanks to Adrian and the other first-alert fish.

HEROES OF THE COAL MINES

You may have heard the phrase "canary in a coal mine." People use it to describe a small early sign of a much bigger problem. For instance, some people say California's fire problem is a canary in a coal mine for what the rest of the country might face as climate change gets worse.

Like many sayings, this one is based in real life. Just as bluegill fish currently watch out for our water, coal miners once brought canaries deep underground to warn of impending danger.

Mines are hazardous places. Underground digging can release carbon monoxide, an invisible, odorless gas that's highly flammable and harmful to breathe. (You almost definitely have a carbon monoxide detector in your house right now.) In the late 1800s and early 1900s, people were looking for ways to warn miners when carbon monoxide was building up—and someone thought of canaries.

Canaries are small yellow birds who love to sing. And just like bluegills, they're very sensitive to chemical changes in their environment. When they're exposed to carbon monoxide, they quiet down, get unsteady on their feet, and may even faint. If miners brought canaries underground, they would know if carbon monoxide was building up.

Miners in the United States and England quickly adopted these **BELLWETHER** birds. Special cages with oxygen tanks attached were designed so that the birds could be revived if they did get into trouble. Suddenly the gloomy mine shafts were full of fluffy, warbling canaries.

BELLWETHER: an early sign that something will happen. (This word also comes from an animal—in this case, the ram at the front of a flock of sheep who, in some shepherding traditions, wears a bell and leads the others.)

Most coal miners loved their canary companions. The United States Bureau of Mines called them "hero birds." One of their biggest jobs was accompanying rescue teams to save miners who had been trapped by explosions or other accidents. A canary named Baldy was famous for helping with five different rescue missions. When he died in the line of duty in 1921, one news service described him as "probably the most valuable employee the Bureau ever had."

But some people wondered if there was a better way. Was it right to take birds deep underground and put them at risk? After all, you can't really ask canaries what they want to do. The same goes for bluegills, who have to spend their shifts alone in very small tanks and occasionally die in spill events.

Over the decades, technology such as electronic carbon monoxide sensors replaced these brave birds. But their legacy lives on in our language. Maybe someday, if technology advances enough to put first-alert fish out of work, we'll start using the phrase "bluegill in a water tank."

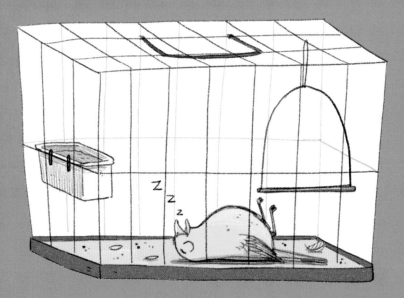

ACTIVITY
CONCENTRATION CHALLENGE

Bluegills can detect a very small amount of something, good or bad, in the water around them. How do you measure up?

YOU'LL NEED:

- 1 liter of clean drinking water
- a straw
- a set of measuring spoons and cups, or a baking scale
- some sugar
- a stirring spoon
- paper and a pencil

1. Sip a little bit of water through the straw to get a baseline taste.

2. Using the measuring spoon or baking scale, add an eighth of a teaspoon or .5 grams of sugar to the water. (You can use a quarter-teaspoon and fill it halfway.)

3. Taste again. Can you tell the difference?

4. If not, keep adding and then tasting, a teeny-tiny bit at a time. Take notes to keep track of how much you've added.

5. When the water finally tastes sweet enough to detect, calculate how much sugar is in there. For reference, a bluegill can detect 50 micrograms of a chemical in one liter of water. That's about a five-thousandth of a teaspoon—or one-twelfth of one grain of sugar!

BONUS

Try again—with salt this time. (You may want to start with an even smaller amount.) Is it easier or harder to detect?

CHAPTER 6
DYNAMITE DOLPHINS

WHEN THE MILITARY NEEDS TO FIND THINGS UNDERWATER, THEY CALL ON THE OCEAN'S MOST ELITE FORCES.

OFF THE COAST OF SAN DIEGO, Jaime Bratis leans over the side of her boat, looks across the steady sea, and waits for her crew member Ten to return. Jaime is a marine mammal scientist with the US Navy, and Ten is out searching for a fake explosive that Jaime's team has dropped in the ocean.

Ten and all of Jaime's other crew members are truly exceptional—they're stronger and faster than any other military divers, they're always eager to train, and they find lost things underwater far more efficiently than the most sophisticated technologies can. That's because they're all sea animals—Jaime's squad includes about eighty bottlenose dolphins.

In the US Navy Marine Mammal Program, dolphins work alongside naval teams to locate things, and sometimes people, that are tough for humans to spot in the deep, murky ocean. They have sharp eyes, but they also have a separate sense that helps them find their way in places that are almost completely

JAIME BRATIS CONDUCTS AN OPEN-WATER TRAINING SESSION WITH A BOTTLENOSE DOLPHIN.

dark. This sense is called **ECHOLOCATION**, and it gives dolphins the ability to navigate, hunt, and find objects in turbulent seas. In the wild, dolphins echolocate to find food, friends, and mates, but they can also be trained to put their echolocation talents to use helping humans.

Navy dolphins are born in navy breeding colonies and raised in groups by their mothers and military trainers. Once they're fully trained, they may be deployed to find underwater explosives that are left over from conflicts that ended years ago, to track down equipment military teams drop from planes to practice hitting targets in the sea, or to prevent unauthorized people from swimming near military harbors and ships.

Like their human counterparts, navy dolphins do a lot of training exercises. Every morning Jaime loads her boat with buckets of fish, then takes one of the dolphins out to sea, where they get down to the hard business of preparing for military missions.

ECHOLOCATION: the process of emitting sound waves and using the echoes reflected back to determine the positions of things

THE SEA SQUAD AT WORK

For Ten, a typical day starts at the seaside naval base where she lives in Point Loma, California. After a fishy breakfast and a quick health check, navy trainers fit a harness around her body, just under her flippers. This harness is outfitted with a tracking device that allows Jaime's team to follow Ten's movements when she's out in the open ocean.

Once she's suited up, Ten is ready to head out to the spot in the ocean where she'll train today. She'll need to travel by boat to get there. Jaime parks her small speedboat right next to the netted bay enclosure where Ten lives.

Jaime's boat is equipped with a contraption that looks like a big padded tray with hinged sides. The navy team unfolds the tray and slides the bottom

A NAVY DOLPHIN ON A TRANSPORT PAD

DOLPHINS CAN FLY,
BUT SHOULD THEY?

For navy dolphins, travel is the hardest part of the job. When called into action, dolphins may have to go hundreds or even thousands of miles away from their base in California, all the way to Canada, Eastern Europe, or Southeast Asia.

For long trips, dolphins are hoisted into fiberglass tanks filled with water to keep them as comfortable as possible. The tanks then get loaded onto trucks, helicopters, and boats. Dolphins are trained for months, sometimes years, to be able to make these trips. Navy veterinarians constantly watch the flippered passengers to make sure that their breathing stays steady and they don't show signs of being anxious or sick. But even though they're being transported in water tanks, trucks and helicopters aren't a dolphin's natural habitat.

There is debate about whether raising dolphins to do military work and make these stressful journeys is cruel. While some animals, like dogs, have long been **DOMESTICATED**, dolphins haven't.

NAVY DOLPHINS IN
TRANSPORT TANKS
ABOARD MILITARY
AIRCRAFT

DOMESTICATED: bred over thousands of years to live and work with humans

Plus there's the issue of consent: these dolphins don't have a choice about whether they want to work with the military, and they face some risks to do their jobs. The navy's Marine Mammal Program also trains California sea lions to retrieve underwater objects, and people ask these questions about them, too.

Animal advocacy groups have long criticized the navy for depriving animals of their natural homes by keeping them in enclosed spaces, for conducting experiments and training exercises that sometimes cause them stress, and for preventing them from learning how to survive in the wild. They point to lots of research showing that dolphins raised in captivity have shorter average life spans than those of wild dolphins.

Navy trainers say that, unlike captive dolphins who live in aquariums and as tourist attractions, navy dolphins live and work in the sea, and "vote with their flippers" when they choose to return home. The dolphins are happy, healthy, and often outlive wild dolphins, they argue, and when the dolphins are no longer able or needed to work, navy veterinarians care for them their entire lives. The dolphins' work also protects humans and marine life. Research conducted on these animals, including more than 1,200 published scientific papers, has increased humans' understanding of the biology and behavior of marine mammals, as well as our knowledge about what kind of care they need.

THIS DOLPHIN IS WEARING A RUBBER EYECUP BLINDFOLD AND AN ACOUSTIC TRANSMITTER FOR ECHOLOCATION RESEARCH.

Which side is right? Are they both right, or neither? Questions about the best ways to treat animals in work and in research are tough and often don't have clear answers. What do *you* think? Should dolphins fly?

over the edge of the enclosure and into Ten's pen, creating a ramp from the enclosure into the boat. They spray water on the padded ramp to make it slick. Ten thrusts her slippery body up onto the mat, then the team pulls the tray, now with a dolphin on top, fully into the boat and folds the sides of the tray up around Ten to form a snug, triangular dolphin house.

Soon they're off, cruising through the open sea. The triangular cocoon keeps Ten stable and out of the sun. During the boat ride, someone from Jaime's team sits by Ten, hosing her off and feeding her fish as they go.

Once they get about forty-five minutes from the shore, Jaime's team unfolds the tray, lifts the mat, and carefully slides Ten into the sea. The team has already gone out earlier that morning and hidden several simulators

THIS DOLPHIN MARKS AN OBJECT ON THE OCEAN FLOOR.

that look like real mines in different locations throughout these waters. Now Ten is on the hunt to find them.

These simulators are designed to replicate underwater mines filled with explosives. Real sea mines are bombs that sit underwater and explode when enemy ships or submarines pass by. Because mines are cheap to produce, easy to deploy, and hard to detect, they're often used in maritime conflicts. But they're also really hard to clean up—so when those conflicts end, mines are often left behind, buried on the seafloor or floating on anchored chains in the water. They can stay there for decades, posing a danger to boats as well as ocean life.

Luckily, Ten is a master mine detector, thanks to her sharp echolocation abilities and Jaime's training. She shoots through the ocean as Jaime cruises alongside, tracking her electronically. Ten scans the water for mines, and Jaime uses GPS to navigate the boat, stopping every now and then at strategic spots along the way. When they reach one of these spots, Jaime uses a hand signal to send Ten off searching for nearby mines. Ten dives and disappears under the water, then comes back up and heads for two round plastic disks that look like Frisbees hanging on the side of Jaime's boat. Ten touches the disk on the left with her nose. That means the area is clear: no simulated mines lurk beneath the surface, and the team can move on.

Several minutes later, Ten dives again. She resurfaces, heads to the side of the boat, and touches the disk on the right, indicating that an imitation mine is nearby. Jaime moves to the back of the boat and hands Ten a device the navy uses to mark where the mines are. The marking device has a small plate attached to it; Ten bites down on the plate, then carries the device straight back to the fake mine. When she releases the marking device, it separates into two pieces—one anchors itself at the bottom of the ocean near the mine, and the other, connected by a long, lightweight line, floats to the surface.

During training, human divers on Jaime's team follow this line down to check Ten's accuracy. If this were a real mission, navy divers would have a few decisions to make. In an active combat scenario, they might simply gather intelligence on the dangerous bomb and leave it there, or they might dispose of it. That often means waiting until Ten has left the scene and the area is clear of people and marine animals, then sending in human divers to carefully place a tiny explosive charge near the mine. This charge essentially breaks and deactivates the mine without actually setting it off. Navy divers detonate the small charge from a safe distance away.

SEARCHING WITH SOUND

Ten specializes in finding mines, but other dolphins in the Marine Mammal Program focus on other tasks, such as spotting swimmers who get too close to areas the navy considers to be dangerous or strategic to a mission. The dolphins get these assignments after Jaime's team has worked with them for several months and gotten to know them individually. "All the dolphins are a little different, and we see what they're good at," Jaime says. They all share one skill: echolocation.

After she dives beneath the surface, Ten starts clicking rapidly. When you make a sound, it usually starts in your vocal cords, then moves past your throat, tongue, and lips. From there, it disperses freely into the air so anyone close by can hear what you have to say, sing, squawk, or squeak. But Ten creates and uses sound very differently, and it starts with her nose.

NAME THAT SOUND

Dolphins use clicks to navigate, but they make other sounds, too. In fact, just as you identify each of your friends by their individual names, dolphins have signature whistles they use to identify one another. Baby dolphins learn their own unique whistle sound from their mothers, and it becomes their sonic calling card for the rest of their lives. If you had to change your name to any sound in the world, what would you choose?

DOLPHINS SEND OUT LOTS OF CLICKS AND NAVIGATE ACCORDING TO HOW LONG IT TAKES THE ECHOES TO RETURN.

Like other dolphins, Ten has two special organs that help her produce and focus sound underwater, explains Dr. Frants Jensen, a scientist at Woods Hole Oceanographic Institution who studies how marine animals echolocate and communicate. The first is called the **PHONIC LIPS**. Phonic lips work very similarly to the way your vocal cords work—air passes over them and they vibrate to make sound waves.

Your vocal cords are located in your throat, but Ten has two sets of phonic lips: one inside each nostril in the nasal passages located at the top of her head, just below her blowhole. Each set does a different job: dolphins use the phonic lips inside their left nostril to make the whistling sounds they use to communicate with other animals, while the ones in the right nostril are used to produce echolocation clicks. Imagine how weird it would be if you used your left nostril to talk and your right nostril to sing or yell!

Two reasons dolphins are so good at using sound waves to navigate dark waters are first, that they can make a lot of echolocation clicks very quickly underwater—somewhere between ten and fifty clicks per second—and second, that they can focus these sound waves into a concentrated beam.

When Ten comes to the surface and breathes in through her blowhole, the air flows into her nasal passages and goes into her lungs. To make an echolocation click, she pushes air from her lungs through the right set of phonic lips and into special air sacs. As she swims through the water, Ten makes echolocation clicks with the air in her lungs first, using muscles in her nasal passages to bounce air back and forth across the phonic lips at lightning speed. When that's gone, the air stored in her air sacs allows her to keep clicking underwater without having to come back up to the surface to take a breath.

Once the sound waves are made, they move from the phonic lips into

TAKE A BREATH

Dolphins can stay underwater for up to ten minutes without coming up for air. For comparison, most people can comfortably hold their breath underwater for only about thirty seconds.

MELON: *a fat-filled organ dolphins use to focus sound waves into a beam*

a fat-filled organ in the front of her head called the **MELON** (the second organ that helps dolphins echolocate). The melon basically acts like a lens and focuses the sound waves into a narrow beam. Instead of sending sound in all directions at once, dolphins can aim their clicks in one specific direction, like the beam of a flashlight.

That skill is crucial, because it means that each click can give Ten information about her aquatic environment. Sound travels really quickly through water—more than four times faster than it does through air of the same

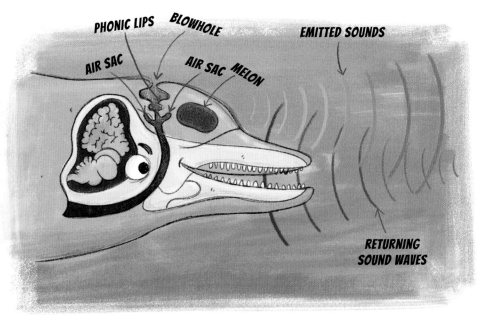

DOLPHINS DON'T JUST CLICK QUICKLY. THEY ALSO AIM THEIR SOUND WAVES INTO BEAMS, ALLOWING THEM TO TARGET A SPECIFIC OBJECT AND GATHER INFO ON HOW FAR AWAY IT IS.

EVOLVING ECHOLOCATION

Dolphins aren't the only creatures that use echolocation. Most bats and some birds also echolocate to detect obstacles and find their way. Bats and dolphins don't have much in common in terms of appearance, behaviors, or habitats. So how did two radically different animals wind up with the exact same super sense? To find the answer, you'll need to jump back a few billion years.

Species change over time. You, for example, have a bigger brain than your ancestors did millions of years ago. Back in cave person days, when food and shelter were hard to come by, bigger brains helped early humans come up with creative ways to find what they needed. Humans with bigger brains were more likely to survive and more likely to have babies compared to those with smaller brains. Over time, there were more babies from parents with bigger brains, and after many, many generations, that big-brain trait eventually became a thing that all humans had.

This process of biological change over long periods of time is called evolution. As members of a species face different challenges, the traits that help them survive those challenges become more common and stick around for generations.

All animals evolve. Dolphins and bats are built differently and live in very different environments, but they both face one common challenge: darkness. Dolphins often live in gray, murky waters. Bats often live in caves, under bridges, or in trees or tunnels where sunlight doesn't reach. They also hunt at night, which helps them avoid predators and birds that compete for food sources.

So even though one of these animals lives underwater and the other on land, being able to navigate through the dark gave both species an evolutionary advantage.

BATS ECHOLOCATE TO FIND FOOD AND NAVIGATE IN THE DARK.

Long ago, the bats and dolphins that were better at echolocation had a higher chance of survival. Millions of years later, that translates to dolphins and bats having super echolocation abilities.

When two different species encounter the same environmental challenge and independently develop similar traits that overcome it, scientists call it **CONVERGENT EVOLUTION**.

CONVERGENT EVOLUTION: when unrelated organisms independently develop similar traits that solve a specific environmental problem

temperature. When Ten targets an underwater object and sends out a click, that sound bounces off the object and echoes back to her within microseconds. With her exceptional hearing, she can figure out how far away that object is by noting how long it took the sound wave to return.

Dolphins use these targeted, rapid-fire echoes to make a detailed mental map of their surroundings that includes where objects are located, their sizes and shapes, and how fast they're moving. After spending months with Jaime learning how to recognize practice mines and receiving fishy treats after finding them during training exercises, Ten can expertly use echolocation clicks to scan a crowded seafloor and find simulated or real explosives hidden among the fish and flotsam.

FROM THE OCEAN TO THE LAB

Ten's trainers harness her skills for military projects, but her humans also want to better understand exactly how her echolocation works. The navy has conducted lots of studies on echolocation and underwater hearing. They're also constantly working to improve their own mine-finding technologies, which use a similar method of mapping through sound, called **SONAR**, a term that stands for **SOUND NAVIGATION AND RANGING**.

But up against dolphins, human-built sonar technologies lose every time. Under ideal ocean conditions, the navy's best mine-finding tech sends out "thousands and thousands and thousands" of sonar pings and crunches the data for about twenty-four hours to identify and pinpoint the location of suspicious objects, says Dr. Mark Xitco, director of the US Navy Marine

SONAR: an echolocation-like system created by humans that uses sound pings to locate objects underwater. The term stands for **SOUND NAVIGATION AND RANGING**.

Mammal Program. "A dolphin can do this with a couple dozen clicks in less than a second."

Since the navy started working with them in 1959, dolphins like Ten have traveled far and wide to do their job, mostly during peacetime. They've blocked swimmers from reaching a pier stocked with US ammunition during the Vietnam War, protected anchored Kuwaiti oil tankers in the late 1980s, and cleared unexploded bombs from former war zones in Eastern Europe.

This work hasn't gone unrecognized. A few navy dolphins have even received medals of achievement. After a long day of mine hunting, Ten returns to Point Loma, where she'll spend her off-hours socializing with other dolphins and enjoying her favorite reward for a job well done—some yummy fish.

A DOLPHIN IN THE US NAVY MARINE MAMMAL PROGRAM

You're missing the fins and flippers, but you can still test out your ability to navigate with sound. Remember, echolocation just means using *echoes* to *locate* where objects are in relation to where you are.

YOU'LL NEED:

- a partner
- a bandana or other blindfold
- a frying pan

1. Put the blindfold on.

2. Ask your partner to take the frying pan and hold it about six inches in front of your face, with the flat bottom facing you.

3. Sing "da da da"—one low note, one medium note, and one high note—and listen to how it sounds.

4. Then ask your partner to move the frying pan really close, only about two inches from your face, and sing again. Can you hear how the pitch changes with the distance?

5. Now have your partner take half a step back (still holding the frying pan up), and sing again. Does the pitch sound different this time?

6. Have your partner take one more half-step back, and try again.

7. Now ask your partner to move the frying pan super close to your face again. The difference in pitch should be clear.

8. Switch, blindfold your partner, and let them hear what it sounds like when you move the frying pan close to their face, one half-step away, then two half-steps away, and back again. If you move closer or farther back, can they guess how far away you are based on how the sound changes?

BONUS Try making different sounds, such as clicking, humming, or animal noises.

CHAPTER 7
COMMUNITY-BUILDING BEES

ON A SUNNY SUMMER DAY in Detroit, Michigan, Justine the honeybee darts between blossoms. She lands on a crabapple flower, then hovers over a red clover, sipping nectar for energy and dusting herself with pollen. When she has gathered enough, she zips back to the hive to deposit her haul—then starts all over.

Justine works for Detroit Hives, a nonprofit organization that's bringing honeybee hives to the city's vacant lots. From dawn till dusk throughout the spring and summer, Justine and her fellow worker bees visit as many blooms as they can, collecting pollen and nectar, which they use to make hundreds of gallons of honey every year.

While they're making honey, they're also doing something even more important. Many plants—including trees that line our streets, flowers that fill our gardens, and fruits and vegetables we eat—need bees to survive. Along with other insects, the Detroit Hives honeybees support the city's plant life, and they're transforming Detroit in the process. The gardens that result from having more bees in the city are slowly replacing abandoned lots, turning desolate blocks into flourishing green spaces.

It's important work. To maximize their efficiency, Justine and the other honeybees call on a source of information that helps them understand flowers on a minute-by-minute basis: electricity.

A LOT OF LOTS

"Busy bees" isn't just an expression. Honeybees are some of the most hard-working animals around, visiting thousands of flowers each day. As they buzz from one plant to another, the bees spread pollen, enabling plants to reproduce. This process is called **POLLINATION**.

Most honeybee species evolved in Africa, but because they're such good pollinators, people have brought them all over the world to help grow crops, from almonds to watermelons. Some beekeepers have hundreds of hives that they drive around in huge trucks so that the bees can work with different crops as they flower. But the bees of Detroit Hives stay in one place and use their pollination power to make their city greener.

Every city has challenges that people are working on. Detroit has a problem with empty space. The city was once one of the most populous in America, home to car manufacturers and other industries that employed hundreds of thousands of people.

POLLINATION: *the process of bringing pollen from one flower to another, which enables the flower to reproduce and develop fruit and seeds*

But in the middle of the twentieth century, factories closed and moved to other

HONEYBEES ARE OFTEN TRANSPORTED
BETWEEN JOBS ON BIG TRUCKS.

countries, and more and more people left the city. Businesses, schools, play-grounds, and homes were shuttered and deserted. People have returned to Detroit, but many of these unused lots and abandoned structures remain—about ninety thousand of them, some estimates say.

When no one takes care of them, vacant lots can fill up with trash. They can make neighborhoods seem empty and sad, so new people and businesses don't want to move in. To fix this problem, some residents are clearing the lots out and building new structures. Other people are making them into art spaces or markets.

BEES NEED YOUR HELP

Recently, some honeybee hives have suffered from "colony collapse disorder"—a syndrome no one quite understands that causes stressed-out worker bees to desert their hives. Honeybees also suffer from other health problems, including mites, viruses, and even poor nutrition, when they don't have access to a variety of flowers. In recent years, honeybee keepers have recorded losses of 30 or even 40 percent of their honeybees.

Native bee populations are also declining, due to habitat loss, pesticides, and sometimes even competition from honeybees. Because native bees are wild animals, not managed like honeybees, it's harder for us to protect them.

So what can you do? You can plant a garden in your backyard, windowsill, roof, or fire escape. Use flowers and other plants that naturally occur in your area to give your local bees a nutritional boost. You can also ask adults in your life to avoid using pesticides and other chemicals outside. Maybe you can even persuade them to leave a little bit of the lawn shaggy and unmown—before too long, you'll have the hottest pollinator restaurant in town.

IN RECENT YEARS, MANY HONEYBEE HIVES HAVE SUFFERED MYSTERIOUS DIE-OFFS.

In 2016, Tim Paule and Nicole Lindsey, the founders of Detroit Hives, had another idea: "How about we try turning a vacant lot into a bee farm?" Tim said. With human help, they thought, honeybees could make the city greener by supporting the growth of healthy plants. They could pollinate flowers and other plants in the lot and in nearby gardens, and even make honey.

FLOWER POWER

To turn unused lots into honeybee havens, Tim and Nicole clean up any trash there and remove invasive plants, leaving wildflowers in place and sometimes planting new ones. When the plants are ready, they bring in beehives, and the

NICOLE LINDSEY IN A BUZZING DETROIT HIVES GARDEN

bees get to work. Justine and her hive mates spend all day zipping from these flowers to the hive and back again, gathering nectar and pollen.

When Justine lands on a flower, she uses her long tongue, or **PROBOSCIS**, to sip a little nectar to get energy. Then she stores the rest of the nectar in a special part of her stomach called the crop. In the process, she also gathers pollen, which clings to pouches on her legs.

Each flower has only a little bit of nectar and pollen, so Justine has to keep moving. Each time she leaves the hive, she visits between fifty and one hundred blossoms. (Imagine having to go to one hundred stores to get everything on your grocery list!)

Because Justine has a limited amount of time and energy each day, she has to prioritize the flowers that are most likely to give her what she needs. Her senses help with this. Justine can smell pollen from far away and can taste nectar with her antennae, mouth, and feet. Her fellow worker bees help her out, too: bees do complicated dance routines, called waggle dances, to tell one another about promising flower patches.

HONEYBEES EXCHANGE INFORMATION BY DANCING.

But sometimes Justine needs even more information to make a decision. That's when she taps into her special super sense.

THE FLOWER IS GIVING OFF A SECRET SIGNAL.

ELECTRIC ATTRACTION

Say Justine is hovering in front of a petunia. It looks and smells great, but there are so many other bees around. If someone already emptied it out, landing on it would be a waste of time. And if she visits too many flowers like that, she could go back to the hive empty-pouched.

Luckily, the flower is giving off a secret signal. We can't sense it, but Justine can. The signal is the plant's **ELECTRIC FIELD**—the pattern of negative electric charges around the flower, explains Dr. Daniel Robert, an expert in bee sensing.

The atoms that make up everything in the universe are made of smaller particles called protons and electrons. If an atom has a balanced number of protons and electrons, it's neutral, meaning it has no electric charge. If it has more electrons than protons, it has a negative charge. If it has more protons than electrons, its charge is positive.

Because of lightning storms that happen high up in the atmosphere, the charge on the Earth's surface is slightly negative. The same goes for things that exist on the surface, including plants. Meanwhile, as bees fly around, the friction they create by flapping their wings and moving through the air makes them lose electrons, leaving them with a positive charge.

When a honeybee lands on a blossom, her positive charge interacts with the flower's negative charge, and changes the electric field around that flower. When Justine arrives, she takes notice. That

ELECTRIC FIELD: the pattern of electric charges around an object

altered electric field acts almost like a SOLD OUT sign, letting her know that another bee has been there and the pollen and nectar are gone. As the flower makes more supplies, the electric field returns to its normal negative state.

Electric fields aren't just for bees—they also help flowers reproduce. Just as with magnets, positive and negative charges attract each other. When Justine lands on a blossom, the negatively charged pollen on the flower is pulled toward the positive charge of her body. Some of it leaps off the flower and sticks right to her.

UGH! SOLD OUT AGAIN!

ELECTRIC FIELD

HONEYBEES SENSE A FLOWER'S ELECTRICAL CHARGE TO FIGURE OUT WHETHER OR NOT IT'S A GOOD TIME TO VISIT.

As Justine flies, she and the pollen she's carrying both lose some electrons to friction. By the time she lands on the next negatively charged flower, the pollen is now positively charged. It jumps away from Justine and onto the new flower, helping to ensure that proper pollination takes place.

All this pollen-leaping happens on a very small scale. Electric charges on individual plants are tiny—billions of times weaker than what it takes to power a lightbulb—and the precise ways that they influence plant and animal behavior aren't well known.

Researchers aren't even sure how bees like Justine detect these charges, although they think it might have something to do with the small, fine hairs that cover their bodies, which vibrate when exposed to electric fields. But there might also be other sensory organs involved, in ways we haven't yet discovered.

HIVE MINDS

Back at the hive, Justine empties out her crop and leg pouches. Other worker bees cart off the supplies—the pollen to feed the hive's larvae, and the nectar to the combs to be made into honey.

Tim and Nicole sell some of this honey to local people and restaurants. They also hire local artists to paint the beehive boxes, and they give tours to school

LOCAL HONEY MADE BY DETROIT HIVES BEES

UNDERWATER ZAPPERS

Like sound, electricity moves through water more efficiently than it does through air. That's why you shouldn't go swimming during a lightning storm. It's also why aquatic animals are much more likely than us landlubbers to have electrical sensing abilities. In fact, sharks, other fish, and even some swimming mammals such as platypuses and dolphins are highly tuned in to electric fields.

Sharks have special organs all over their heads that look like little pores filled with jelly. They're called ampullae of Lorenzini, and they help the sharks detect electricity as well as magnetic fields. Because all animals create electric fields when they move, sharks can use this power to find prey wherever it's hiding. (Some scientists think that this could also be why they occasionally bite through undersea telephone and internet cables—maybe they're attracted to the buzz.)

Lots of fish use electroreception to find one another. But at least one special species, the ghost knife fish, can also use it to communicate. A special organ at the base of this fish's tail produces electric "chirps" of different lengths, which send messages like "I'm over here" or "Let's mate!"

Electroreception isn't just for our finned friends. Platypuses have electric receptors in their bills. When they dive underwater to hunt, they close their eyes, stop up their ears and nostrils, and push their wide, flat bills into the mucky bottoms of streams. The receptors help them tell the difference between tasty snacks like shrimp, which give off an electric signal, and rocks and dirt, which don't.

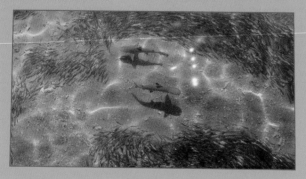

THESE BLACKTIP REEF SHARKS HUNT BY DETECTING ELECTRIC FIELDS.

classes, teaching them about the bees and their important jobs. Neighborhood residents stop by to smell the fresh air, watch the bees at work, and drink tea with honey made right there.

Meanwhile, the flowers Justine visited use the pollen she brought to make fruits, vegetables, and seeds. The air flits with butterflies, bees, and other native pollinators, who do the same job as Justine. As the whole ecosystem gets healthier, the soil fills with ants, spiders, and beetles.

With these insects hard at work, the lot becomes flowery and fragrant, and the whole space gets even greener and more welcoming. Voilà! The vacant lot is no longer vacant. Instead, it's a "habitat for all living things, where everything is thriving," Tim says. And it's all made possible by busy, bzz-y bees.

A VISITOR MEETS SOME BEES AT A DETROIT HIVES GARDEN.

WHO'S WHO IN NATIVE POLLINATORS

Sure, you've heard of honeybees. But what about squash bees, blueberry bees, and yucca moths?

Although these insects don't take up as much of the limelight, they're super important members of their ecosystems. And because they coevolved directly alongside the plants they live with, many are able to pollinate them better than honeybees can. In fact, a lot of experts think we should rely less on shipping honeybees from farm to farm and focus on protecting native pollinators instead. Here are a few particularly phenomenal pollinators worth saluting:

NAME: SQUASH BEE

HOME RANGE: *Throughout the United States and Mexico*

SPECIAL SKILL: Squash bees are great at pollinating squashes, pumpkins, and zucchinis because they're so intimately tied with them—they dig nests right next to their stems, and male bees spend their afternoons sleeping inside their flowers. When Native Americans started cultivating squash about five thousand years ago and then began growing the plants in places across the whole continent, the bees followed.

NAME: ALKALI BEE

HOME RANGE: *The western and southwestern United States*

SPECIAL SKILL: Many plants in the pea family have flowers that work like spring traps: when you apply pressure to a certain petal, the flower snaps open, exposing the pollen. Most bees don't know how to trigger these flowers—but alkali bees do. They're so helpful for pollinating crops like alfalfa that some farmers build them "bee beds" full of salty dirt to encourage them to move in nearby.

NAME: **YUCCA MOTH**

HOME RANGE: *The southwestern United States and Mexico*

SPECIAL SKILL: Yucca moths and yucca plants have a special, interdependent relationship. The female moth uses tentacles around her mouth to scrape pollen out of the center of a yucca flower and into a big ball. Then she carries the pollen ball to another yucca plant. After laying eggs in that flower, she carefully pollinates it to ensure that it will make fruit—which her babies will then eat when they hatch.

NAME: **BLUEBERRY BEE**

HOME RANGE: *The eastern United States and Canada*

SPECIAL SKILL: Some plants, including blueberries, cranberries, and tomatoes, hide their pollen deep inside their flowers. Bees must climb into the flowers and use their powerful wings to vibrate them in exactly the right way so that the pollen shakes out—a trick called **SONICATION**. Blueberry bees know the secret buzz password and keep bushes from Nova Scotia to Georgia full of berries.

NAME: **CHOCOLATE MIDGE**

HOME RANGE: *Central America, South America, Africa, and Asia*

SPECIAL SKILL: Midges are not very popular. They like to bite, swarm around, and buzz in your ears. But without them and some other helpful pollinators, we wouldn't have chocolate! Midges are tiny and numerous enough to crawl into the strangely shaped flowers of the cacao tree and help them swap pollen. Even they aren't great at it—scientists estimate that only one in every five hundred flowers turns into a cacao pod—but we're lucky that they keep trying.

SONICATION: *the use of sound energy to extract materials from plants and algae*

ACTIVITY
POLLEN JUMP

When a positively charged bee lands on a flower, the negatively charged pollen "jumps" onto the bee. You can re-create the same effect at a bigger scale using static electricity.

YOU'LL NEED:

- some dry cereal
- a plate
- a balloon
- a wool sock, sweater, or other woolly material

1. Crush up some of the dry cereal into a powder and put it on the plate.

2. Blow up the balloon.

3. Rub the balloon all over with the wool sock, sweater, or other material. (By doing this, you're transferring loose electrons from the wool and building up a negative electric field around the balloon.)

4. Bring the balloon close to the dry cereal. What happens? How far can you get the powdered cereal to jump?

BONUS

Try this with other small objects, such as confetti flakes, the hairs on your arm, or even a stream of water from the faucet. Get creative! You can "recharge" the balloon as often as you'd like by rubbing it with the wool.

CHAPTER 8
SATELLITE SPECIES

ON THE MORNING of October 30, 2016, Berta the cow woke up in her stable and noticed that something was off. On a typical day, Berta, who lives on a cheese farm in central Italy, would mill around in her stall and munch on a grassy breakfast. But it didn't feel like a typical day. As the people around her began the morning's activities, Berta instead stood perfectly still—and so did all the other dairy cows.

The dogs on the farm also started acting strange. They began pacing and running around. In response, the cows got even more uneasy, stomping and shifting their feet. And then, just a few hours later . . . *BOOM!* An earthquake ripped through the ground below, crumpling houses and historic buildings in the nearest town and sending panicked people rushing into the streets.

From the rest of this book, you know that animals around the world can sense lots of things we can't. People have long wondered whether some of these unique senses might help give animals advance notice of natural disasters such as earthquakes, volcanic eruptions, and tsunamis. If so, listening to their warnings could save lives—but it's hard to know for sure.

So since 2002, researchers working on a project called ICARUS have been putting **TRACKING TAGS** on thousands of animals all around the world, including cows like Berta. By learning to track these animals' movements and interpret their behaviors, researchers hope they'll eventually be able to predict all kinds of events, from earthquakes to disease outbreaks to poaching attempts.

EARTHQUAKE!

People throughout history have noticed that animals seem to be able to sense when earthquakes are coming far in advance. The ancient Greek author Aelian wrote that in the days before a quake destroyed the town of Helice in 373 BCE, "all the mice and martens and snakes and centipedes and beetles and every other creature" fled the area.

Sometimes people heed these warnings. In February 1975, officials in China successfully evacuated much of the city of Haicheng just before a huge earthquake. They were tipped off partly by the many frogs, snakes, and mice that had come out of hibernation early.

How might animals sense earthquakes when instruments invented by humans can't? Researchers have a couple of theories. It's possible that animals can smell gases released from the ground or feel new electric charges in the air with their skin or fur.

But the evidence that they can make these predictions at all is mostly **ANECDOTAL**—meaning that it's derived from stories and incidental observations rather than controlled experiments.

A HISTORY OF ANIMAL TRACKING

CAVE ART DEPICTING A HUNT, FROM THE MAGURA CAVE, IN BULGARIA

Ever since people have existed, we've followed animals. The earliest humans hunted wildebeests and monkeys and may have tracked large carnivores like saber-toothed cats in order to feast on their leftovers. Since then, most cultures around the world have found cause to tail other species, whether that means paddling after narwhals like the Inuit people of Greenland, following wild birds to trees full of honey like the Hadza people of Tanzania, or stalking moose through the forests like the Algonquin people of Canada.

More recently, new ideas and technologies have allowed us to track animals over longer distances and for different reasons. In the early 1900s, people began banding birds—catching them and giving them small metal bracelets stamped with codes that indicate where and when they were found. Banding has helped answer questions about different bird species, including how long they live and how far they migrate. In the 1960s, scientists started putting chunky radio collars on big animals like grizzly bears, using the signals from the collars to figure out where they roam, hang out, and even hibernate.

In the 1970s, scientists designed new collars that beamed data up to satellites and then back down to computers. Researchers could get that information from anywhere. Pinpointing animals' specific locations got even easier a couple of decades later, when Global Positioning System (GPS) satellites first took flight. But these innovations piggybacked off of technology that was made for other purposes. ICARUS is the first project with its own dedicated transmission antenna, specifically designed to work with animal trackers.

In order to figure out whether animals actually know when earthquakes are coming, scientists have to keep a close eye on them and compare their normal behavior to how they act just before a quake hits. That's where ICARUS comes in.

TAG, YOU'RE IT

The name ICARUS stands for International Cooperation for Animal Research Using Space, and it's the largest project in the world aimed at figuring out where animals go and what they do. It was created by a scientist named Dr. Martin Wikelski about twenty years ago with the goal of tracking more species than ever before and gathering all the data in one place.

Martin and his team have designed lightweight tracking tags that can withstand all the running, crawling, flying, and swimming that make up an animal's day. "We call them wearables for wildlife," he says.

The tags fit on animals like necklaces or bracelets. They're equipped with GPS locators, which track where the animals are, and **ACCELEROMETERS**, which figure out how fast and in what direction they're moving.

Some tags even have temperature and pressure sensors that gather information about the animals' health and their surrounding environments. They are also solar-powered, so they recharge whenever the animal is in the sun.

Each tag beams its own stream of information to an antenna on the International Space Station as it orbits overhead. There, the individual streams are compiled into one big data stream and sent back to a computer at ICARUS headquarters in Moscow. The information is uploaded to a global database called Movebank, where researchers and other interested people can analyze

ACCELEROMETER: *a sensor that can tell how fast and in what direction it is moving*

COSMONAUT SERGEY PROKOPYEV INSTALLS THE ANTENNA
USED BY ICARUS ON THE INTERNATIONAL SPACE STATION.

it. By consistently tracking the movements of animals, scientists can see when those movements change.

After a series of earthquakes shook up central Italy in the summer of 2016, Martin Wikelski and another ICARUS scientist, Uschi Müller, traveled there to put tags on Berta and other cows, dogs, and sheep. Thanks to the tags, they were able to learn each animal's daily routine—how much they moved and how far they roamed. After another major earthquake hit on October 30 of that year, they had enough data to easily compare how the animals acted on normal mornings to how they acted the day of the quake.

They found a huge difference. Berta and the other cows were much more still, and the dogs more frenzied. This started about six hours before

TRACK STARS

Satellite tracking helps us understand how entire species behave. But individual animals have also taught us a lot by wearing tracking bands, tags, and collars. Here are some of the most notable participants in the history of animal tracking studies.

MONIQUE, THE SPACE ELK: In 1970, scientists hoping to learn more about elk migration in Wyoming designed the first-ever satellite tracking collar. They fastened it to an elk they named Monique. (Newspapers started calling her Monique the Space Elk.) The device weighed twenty-three pounds—as much as two gallons of paint—but it didn't bother Monique. She wore it and proved that the technology worked, setting the tone for a new era of tracking studies.

FISHER, THE SPOT-ON LOGGERHEAD TURTLE: In 1995, researchers found a sick loggerhead sea turtle on a beach in North Carolina. They named him Fisher and cared for him in a local aquarium for ten years until he was ready to go back to the wild. They placed a tag on him and set him free in the Atlantic Ocean, wondering where he would decide to go after so long in captivity. To their surprise, Fisher headed straight to the islands of Cape Verde: the same place thousands of other sea turtles were gathering to mate.

MR. NICK, THE INTERNATIONAL ELEPHANT: In 1997, elephant researchers in Kenya were running into a problem. All elephants are protected in Kenya, but some study subjects were getting injured or killed. Researchers thought that they might be crossing the border into Tanzania, where hunting them is legal. To prove it, researchers outfitted two elephants with GPS collars and found that one, Mr. Nick, did cross back and forth frequently. To protect the research, the Tanzanian government made elephant hunting off-limits in the places where Mr. Nick and other border crossers liked to hang out.

MARY LEE, THE SHARK WHO TWEETED: In 2012, an ocean research group called OCEARCH tagged a great white shark they named Mary Lee and made her general location visible on their website.

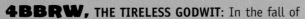

For the next five years, people tracked Mary Lee's every move as she swam from Florida to New York to New Jersey. Someone even made her a Twitter account, but her fame didn't last long. In 2017, Mary Lee's tag stopped pinging, most likely because its battery died.

4BBRW, THE TIRELESS GODWIT: In the fall of 2021, a group of pigeon-size shorebirds with bands on their legs took off from the coast of Alaska and headed south. Ten days later, these birds, called bar-tailed godwits, touched down all the way across the world in Australia. One godwit, known as 4BBRW for the sequence of bands on his leg, set a new nonstop flight record, winging 8,100 miles without stopping at all, not even for a nap.

the earthquake hit, and similar patterns played out in advance of smaller earthquakes that occurred that fall. What's more, the animals seemed to feed off one another's reactions—their unusual behavior became even more pronounced when they could see that their friends had been thrown off as well.

In 2011, Martin and Uschi did a similar experiment with goats living on the sides of volcanoes. They found the same kind of pattern: in the hours before an eruption, all the normally mild-mannered goats began running up and down the slope and hiding under bushes and trees.

In both cases, each individual animal's response was interesting on its own. But combined, they "make this sixth sense," Martin says. All together, they provided the most convincing evidence yet that animals can sense natural disasters long before people can.

STRENGTH IN NUMBERS

Martin wants to go big . . . and little. To increase the amount of ICARUS data available to researchers around the world, his team is working to shrink the tags so that lighter creatures like small songbirds can wear them—and maybe eventually even bees and butterflies. (Right now, the smallest tags are half the size of a postage stamp and weigh the same as three paper clips.)

Researchers are already using the existing tags to dig into scientific questions about animal migrations—where different species go and when. They've tagged endangered saiga antelopes in Russia in order to more effectively protect their habitat, blackbirds to see whether climate change is affecting their migration, and baby Galápagos tortoises to learn where they spend their early years.

GOATS BEGAN RUNNING UP AND DOWN THE SLOPE.

SHOULD WE SNOOP ON ANIMALS?

It's easier than ever to spy on wild animals. You can find livestreams of aquarium penguins diving and waddling, zoo elephants swinging their trunks, and even wild brown bears catching salmon. Motion-triggered camera traps capture footage of curious backyard raccoons and prowling jungle leopards.

Tracking and observing animals can help us determine where they live and travel so we can protect those places. It also helps us figure out what they need, so we can better safeguard those things in the wild and provide them in our zoos, aquariums, and labs. And following individual creatures can make us care about their health and happiness, so that they're less like a data point and more like a friend.

But some experts think that we're taking things a bit too far. Carrying tracking tags has been shown to stress out certain species, although better tag designs reduce this risk. Turning cows and goats into earthquake and disease detectors could actually make us more likely to think of them as tools rather than as living beings. And privacy is important to people—maybe it's important to animals, too. (Imagine if adults in your life could watch you every moment of every day!)

So what do you think: Should we keep snooping on animals? Or should we sometimes act like there's a Do Not Disturb sign up?

THE PANDA CAMS AT THE SMITHSONIAN'S NATIONAL ZOO KEEP AN EYE ON THE GIANT PANDAS.

A DUKE UNIVERSITY MARINE LAB RESEARCHER TAGS
A PILOT WHALE OFF THE COAST OF HAWAII.

Martin and his collaborators are starting to use the technology to manage tough global problems, too. For example, many of history's worst disease outbreaks, including the Covid-19 pandemic, began in animals. Experts are now using ICARUS to monitor the health of different populations, including wild bats and ducks. This way, we're more likely to discover illness when it develops, he says. We might even be able to stop viruses before they cross over from animals to people.

Tracking data is also useful to conservationists, even in cases where it's not a good idea to directly track an endangered animal. Black rhinoceroses, for instance, are critically endangered, in part because poachers kill them for their horns. Tagging the rhinos themselves can only alert the rangers that the animals are in danger after they've already been poached. So instead, rangers in Kruger National Park, in South Africa, are starting to tag other animals, such as gazelles, zebras, and giraffes, and are building a system that will use ICARUS to keep track of them. When these animals run from an intruder, their movements will serve as a warning to park rangers that poachers are coming.

The ICARUS team is also still watching Berta. After the initial earthquake study, the researchers kept the tags on her and a few other animals. Now, every three minutes, the barnyard's movements are sent to ICARUS headquarters. If the animals start behaving oddly, an alarm goes off. Before a minor earthquake in 2019, the animals successfully gave the scientists a "good pre-warning," Martin says.

These systems still need a lot more testing before they can be implemented on a wide scale. But in the future, teams of tagged animals across the world might save people's lives just by living their own.

A SMALL TRANSMITTER TAG WORN BY AN ORCHID BEE

ACTIVITY
A DAY IN THE LIFE

So . . . what *do* animals do all day? A creature log can help you figure it out.

YOU'LL NEED:

- a pet, a backyard squirrel, or other local animal that you can observe, or a smartphone or computer to observe an animal online
- a notebook
- a pen or pencil
- a stopwatch

1. Pick an animal to focus on. Maybe it's a dog, a squirrel that visits your bird feeder every day, or a member of an anthill in your backyard. (No animals in your daily life? Check out a livestream from a zoo or wildlife camera. Some favorites include the penguin cam and elephant cam at the San Diego Zoo and the Brooks Falls brown bear cam at explore.org.)

2. Observe your animal for five minutes. Write down the time, their location, and what

they're doing. Are they sleeping? Eating? Exploring?
For how long? Use your stopwatch for precision.

3. Do a five-minute observation a few times during the
day. (If your animal has disappeared, write that down,
and think of it as an opportunity—what might they
be doing now?)

4. At the end of the day, reread your creature log.
Do you have a better understanding of this animal's
life? Write down any patterns you found and any new
questions you have now. Can you chart their activities
or map their daily journey?

BONUS #1

Do it again tomorrow! Or try observing your
animal for five minutes every day for as long
as you can. Then you can answer even bigger
questions—for instance, does that squirrel act
differently in the spring versus the fall?

Great science often comes from a mix of data
and imagination. What happens if, instead of
sticking to strict observations, you try to put
yourself in the animal's place or even write
from their perspective? What can you learn
from each approach, and what gets left out?
Is there a way to combine the two?

BONUS #2

FOR FURTHER EXPLORATION

IN THIS BOOK, you've met animals with lots of different super senses, from chemical-detecting fish to whiskery ferrets. And you've seen the things they do for people, from delivering messages to predicting natural disasters.

All these collaborations involve a different kind of super sense: human curiosity. Our desire to learn more about our fellow creatures has led us to investigate how they experience the world and to apply their skills and biologies to our own goals.

As you've seen, this work comes with complications—questions about whether it's ethical for us to enlist animals to do these jobs and what our responsibilities are toward these species who help us so much. This is especially true when the problems they help solve, from pollution to discarded war weaponry, were caused by human decisions.

The examples in this book barely scratch the surface of what animals can do and whom they could help. This book focuses mostly on America and Europe, but there are human-animal partnerships all over the world—from fishers in Brazil who work with dolphins to catch mullets, to librarians in Pakistan who use camels to transport books across the desert. We've tried to highlight examples you might not have heard of before, but there are a lot that are probably more familiar, such as guide dogs who help people with visual impairments get around.

If you're interested in learning more about the topics in the book, we've provided a list of general resources for you to explore, as well as a topic-by-topic list of specific resources. We had so much fun doing the research for this book, and we hope you have fun exploring further!

General Resources

Bedell, J. M. *So, You Want to Work with Animals?* New York: Aladdin, 2017.

Gill, Nic. *Animal Eco-Warriors: Humans and Animals Working Together to Protect Our Planet.* Clayton South, Victoria, Australia: CSIRO, 2017.

Keim, Brandon. *Inside Animal Minds: What They Think, Feel, and Know.* Single-issue magazine. Washington, DC: National Geographic Society, 2017.

Keim, Brandon. *Secrets of Animal Communication.* Single-issue magazine. Washington, DC: National Geographic Society, 2019.

King, Barbara J. *Animals' Best Friends: Putting Compassion to Work for Animals in Captivity and the Wild.* Chicago: University of Chicago Press, 2021.

Morell, Virginia. *Animal Wise: The Thoughts and Emotions of Our Fellow Creatures.* New York: Crown, 2013.

Scientists in the Field. Book series. Boston: HMH Books.

Swanbeck, Steve. *The Seeing Eye.* Charleston, SC: Arcadia, 2002.

Chapter 1: Detector Dogs

Eba the Dog and Dr. Giles's Work

"Center for Conservation Biology." University of Washington Center for Conservation Biology. Accessed October 10, 2020. https://conservationbiology.uw.edu.

Dog Olfaction

Handwerk, Brian. "In Some Ways, Your Sense of Smell Is Actually Better Than a Dog's." *Smithsonian,* May 22, 2017. https://www.smithsonianmag.com/science-nature/you-actually-smell-better-dog-180963391.

Horowitz, Alexandra. *Being a Dog: Following the Dog into a World of Smell.* New York: Scribner, 2016.

Tyson, Peter. "Dogs' Dazzling Sense of Smell." *NOVA*, October 4, 2012. https://www.pbs.org /wgbh/nova/article/dogs-sense-of-smell.

Whale Poop and Earwax

Hooper, Rowan. "Sperm Whale's Emergency Evacuation . . . of Its Bowels." *New Scientist*, January 28, 2015. https://www.newscientist.com/article/mg22530064-700-sperm-whales -emergency-evacuation-of-its-bowels.

Yong, Ed. "The History of the Oceans Is Locked in Whale Earwax." *Atlantic*, November 21, 2018. https://www.theatlantic.com/science/archive/2018/11/astonishing-history-locked-whale -earwax/576349.

Other Detector Dogs

"Amamigunto National Park Efforts." Government of Japan, Ministry of the Environment. Accessed March 21, 2021. https://www.env.go.jp/en/nature/nps/park/amami/effort.html.

"Medical Detection Dogs." Medical Detection Dogs. Accessed March 21, 2021. https://www .medicaldetectiondogs.org.uk.

"Stop the Trafficking." Africa Wildlife Foundation. Accessed March 21, 2020. https://www .awf.org/stop-trafficking.

Yee, Amy. "How These Dogs Protect Elephants." *National Geographic*, April 27, 2016. https: //www.nationalgeographic.com/animals/article/160427-kenya-wildlife-service-sniffer -dogs-smuggled-ivory-airport-port-elephant-poaching.

Chapter 2: Fast Ferrets

Cynthia and Other Working Ferrets

"Working Ferrets." National Ferret School. Accessed October 30, 2020. https://ferretbusiness .honeybank.com/working-ferrets.

Whisker Sensory Systems

Braczkowski, Alexander Richard. "Curious Kids: Why Do Tigers Have Whiskers?" *The Conversation*, April 4, 2019. https://theconversation.com/curious-kids-why-do-tigers -have-whiskers-110791.

Pochron, Sharon. "By a Whisker." *Science News for Students*, September 2, 2012. https://www .sciencenewsforstudents.org/article/whisker.

Stetka, Bret. "Seals Use Their Whiskers to See and Hear." *Atlantic*, October 30, 2015. https://www .theatlantic.com/science/archive/2015/10/seals-use-their-whiskers-to-see-and-hear/413269.

Catfish Barbels

Nuwer, Rachel. "This Catfish's Whiskers Are Like Ultra-Sensitive pH Strips." *Smithsonian*, June 5, 2014. https://www.smithsonianmag.com/science-nature/catfish-whiskers -are-ultra-sensitive-ph-strips-180951665/.

Felicia the Particle Accelerator Ferret

Beck, Frank. "Felicia Helps Out." Fermilab News, October 5, 2016. https://news.fnal .gov/2016/10/felicia-helps-out/.

Pinkowski, Jen. "Why Physicists Tried to Put a Ferret in a Particle Accelerator." *Atlas Obscura*, April 2, 2019. https://www.atlasobscura.com/articles/felicia-ferret-particle-accelerator -fermilab.

Chapter 3: Special Delivery Pigeons

Rocky Mountain Adventures and Pigeon Express

Inscoe, Michael. "The Pigeon Express." *Atlas Obscura*, September 29, 2017. https://www .atlasobscura.com/places/pigeon-express.

"RMA Pigeon Story." *Rocky Mountain Adventures*, February 22, 2021. https://www.shoprma .com/articles/rma-pigeon-story/.

Stookesberry, Ben. "Pigeon Express." *Vimeo*, July 29, 2018. https://vimeo.com/5558263.

Pigeon Navigation

Blechman, Andrew D. *Pigeons: The Fascinating Saga of the World's Most Revered and Reviled Bird*. St. Lucia: University of Queensland Press, 2007.

Mancini, Mark. "15 Incredible Facts about Pigeons." *Mental Floss*, April 19, 2018. https:// www.mentalfloss.com/article/535506/facts-about-pigeons.

Peterson, Todd. "Homing Pigeons." *BirdNote*. https://www.birdnote.org/listen/shows /homing-pigeons.

Pigeon Messengers through History

"Cher Ami." Smithsonian Institution, National Museum of Natural History. Smithsonian ID no. AF.30714, accession no. 65695. https://www.si.edu/object/nmah_425415.

Dash, Mike. "Closing the Pigeon Gap." *Smithsonian*, April 17, 2012. https://www.smithsonianmag.com/history/closing-the-pigeon-gap-68103438/.

Eschner, Kat. "This New Zealand Island's Pigeon Mail Stamps Are Still Prized." *Smithsonian*, November 1, 2017. https://www.smithsonianmag.com/smart-news/new-zealand-islands-pigeon-mail-stamps-are-still-prized-180965342/.

Giaimo, Cara. "France's Lost Pigeon-and-Balloon Memorial Is Well Worth Remembering." *Atlas Obscura*, November 16, 2017. http://www.atlasobscura.com/articles/pigeon-balloon-memorial-paris-bartholdi.

Marsh, Alison. "Consider the Pigeon, a Surprisingly Capable Technology." *IEEE Spectrum*, March 29, 2019. https://spectrum.ieee.org/tech-history/silicon-revolution/consider-the-pigeon-a-surprisingly-capable-technology.

Magnetic Sensing in Other Animals

Barrie, David, and Neil Gower. *Supernavigators: Exploring the Wonders of How Animals Find Their Way.* New York: Experiment, 2020.

Hand, Eric. "Maverick Scientist Thinks He Has Discovered a Magnetic Sixth Sense in Humans." *Science*, June 23, 2016. https://www.sciencemag.org/news/2016/06/maverick-scientist-thinks-he-has-discovered-magnetic-sixth-sense-humans.

Klein, JoAnna. "Magnetic Sense Helps Billions of Moths on an Australian Migration." *New York Times*, June 21, 2018. https://www.nytimes.com/2018/06/21/science/moths-magnetic-australia.html.

"Magnetoreception." Lohmann Lab, University of North Carolina at Chapel Hill. Accessed May 12, 2021. https://lohmannlab.web.unc.edu/magnetoreception/.

Chapter 4: Gobbling Goats

California Wildfires and Firenadoes

Glick, Molly. "What Makes a Firenado?" *Sierra*, August 25, 2020. https://www.sierraclub.org/sierra/what-makes-firenado.

Pierre-Louis, Kendra, and John Schwartz. "Why Does California Have So Many Wildfires?" *New York Times*, June 16, 2021. https://www.nytimes.com/article/why-does-california-have-wildfires.html.

Sweeney, Don. "Glass Fire Burned 1 Acre Every 5 Seconds in California. How Fast Can Wildfires Grow?" *Sacramento Bee*, September 29, 2020. https://www.sacbee.com/news/california/fires/article246092930.html.

Butterflies That Need Fire

Couch, Christina. "These Super Rare Butterflies Thrive on Army Bases. The U.S. Military Is Helping Them." *NOVA Next*, April 17, 2019. https://www.pbs.org/wgbh/nova/article/butterflies-department-of-defense.

Fire Practices among Indigenous Peoples

Cagle, Susie. "'Fire Is Medicine': The Tribes Burning California Forests to Save Them." *Guardian*, November 21, 2019. https://www.theguardian.com/us-news/2019/nov/21/wildfire-prescribed-burns-california-native-americans.

"Indigenous Peoples Burning Network." Nature Conservancy Conservation Gateway. Accessed May 10, 2021. http://www.conservationgateway.org/ConservationPractices/FireLandscapes/Pages/IPBN.aspx.

Steinbring, Scot. "Wildland Fire Program." Karuk Tribe official website. Accessed May 10, 2021. https://www.karuk.us/index.php/departments/natural-resources/eco-cultural-revitalization/wildland-fire-program.

Tannins and Goat Saliva

"Tannins." U.S. Forest Service. Accessed June 3, 2021. https://www.fs.fed.us/wildflowers/ethnobotany/tannins.shtml.

Invasive and Native Species

"Green Invaders." *National Geographic Kids*. Accessed October 14, 2020. https://kids.nationalgeographic.com/science/article/green-invaders.

"Invasive Non-Native Species." U.S. Environmental Protection Agency. Accessed October 14, 2020. https://www.epa.gov/watershedacademy/invasive-non-native-species.

Lobsters' Unusual Anatomy

"Lobsters Pee Out of Where?" *New England Aquarium Exhibit Galleries* (blog), November 13, 2015. http://galleries.neaq.org/2015/11/lobsters-pee-out-ofwhere.html.

The Relationship between Smell and Taste

Small, Dana. "How Does the Way Food Looks or Its Smell Influence Taste?" *Scientific American*, April 2, 2008. https://www.scientificamerican.com/article/experts-how-does-sight-smell-affect-taste.

Chapter 5: First-Alert Fish

Blue Sources and Other Fish Monitoring Systems

"How Does a Bluegill Act Like a Canary?" Blue Sources. Accessed April 1, 2021. https://www.bluesources.com/#about.

Lee, Christopher. "Bluegill on Guard in Region's Water Supply." *Washington Post*, September 18, 2006. https://www.washingtonpost.com/archive/politics/2006/09/18/bluegill-on-guard-in-regions-water-supply/e6331e99-e447-49a8-b329-fd3a572c1966/.

Mongilio, Heather. "Frederick Company to Expand on Fort Detrick Fish Biomonitoring System." *Frederick (MD) News-Post*, March 2, 2019. https://www.fredericknewspost.com/news/science_and_technology/frederick-company-to-expand-on-fort-detrick-fish-biomonitoring-system/article_9c7780ec-c553-53fc-9ea4-cb607d6dd120.html.

Water Pollution in the Potomac

Diemand, Melissa, ed. "2020 Potomac River Report Card." Potomac Conservancy, October 20, 2020. https://potomacreportcard.org/.

How Fish Sense

Balcombe, Jonathan. *What a Fish Knows: The Inner Lives of Our Underwater Cousins*. New York: Scientific American/Farrar, Straus, and Giroux, 2016.

Spencer, Erin. "How Do Gills Work?" *Ocean Currents* (blog). Ocean Conservancy, January 17, 2020. https://oceanconservancy.org/blog/2020/01/17/gills/.

Canaries and Other First-Alert Animals

Gale Ambassadors. "Canaries in the Coal Mine." *Gale Review* (blog). Gale International, September 8, 2020. https://review.gale.com/2020/09/08/canaries-in-the-coal-mine/.

Micu, Alexandru. "In Poznan, Poland, Eight Clams Get to Decide If People in the City Get Water or Not." ZME Science, December 28, 2020. https://www.zmescience.com/science/poznan-mussel-water-plants-892524/.

Chapter 6: Dynamite Dolphins

Navy Dolphins and Ethical Questions about Them

Gilliland, Haley Cohen. "A Brief History of the US Navy's Dolphins." *MIT Technology Review*, October 24, 2019. https://www.technologyreview.com/2019/10/24/306/dolphin-echolocation-us-navy-war.

"The Story of the Navy Dolphins." *Frontline*. Accessed June 1, 2020. https://www.pbs.org/wgbh/pages/frontline/shows/whales/etc/navycron.html.

"U.S. Navy Marine Mammal Program." Naval Information Warfare Center Pacific (NWIC Pacific). Accessed July 22, 2020. https://www.niwcpacific.navy.mil/marine-mammal-program.

Zeldovich, Lina. "The Great Dolphin Dilemma." *Hakai*, February 5, 2019. https://www.hakaimagazine.com/features/the-great-dolphin-dilemma.

Underwater Mines Left Over after War

Noack, Rick. "Estonia Is Still Clearing Thousands of World War II Mines from Its Waters." *Washington Post*, October 26, 2018. https://www.washingtonpost.com/world/2018/10/26/estonia-mines.

Echolocation and Underwater Sound

De Brabandere, Sabine. "What Do You Hear Underwater?" *Scientific American*, June 27, 2019. https://www.scientificamerican.com/article/what-do-you-hear-underwater.

Langley, Liz. "Echolocation Is Nature's Built-in Sonar. Here's How It Works." *National Geographic*, February 3, 2021. https://www.nationalgeographic.com/animals/article/echolocation-is-nature-built-in-sonar-here-is-how-it-works.

Morell, Virginia. "Dolphins Can Call Each Other, Not by Name, But by Whistle." *Science*, February 20, 2013. https://www.sciencemag.org/news/2013/02/dolphins-can-call-each-other-not-name-whistle.

Dolphins and People Holding Their Breath

Hecker, Bruce. "How Do Whales and Dolphins Sleep Without Drowning?" *Scientific American*, February 2, 1998. https://www.scientificamerican.com/article/how-do-whales-and-dolphin/.

Palmer, Brian. "How Long Can You Hold Your Breath?" *Slate*, November 18, 2013. https://slate
.com/technology/2013/11/nicholas-mevoli-freediving-death-what-happens-to-people
-who-practice-holding-their-breath.html.

Sonar and Biosonar

Au, Whitlow W. L. "History of Dolphin Biosonar Research." *Acoustics Today* 11, no. 4
(Fall 2015): 11–17. https://acousticstoday.org/wp-content/uploads/2015/11/Dolphin
-Biosonar-Research.pdf.

Convergent Evolution

Yong, Ed. "Echolocation in Bats and Whales Based on Same Changes to Same Gene." *National
Geographic*, January 25, 2010. https://www.nationalgeographic.com/science/article
/echolocation-in-bats-and-whales-based-on-same-changes-to-same-gene.

Chapter 7: Community-Building Bees

Detroit Hives

"About Us." Detroit Hives. Accessed May 11, 2021. https://detroithives.org/about-us/.

Davis, Kathleen, and Ira Flatow. "So You Wanna Be a Beekeeper?" *Science Friday*, April 2,
2021. https://www.sciencefriday.com/segments/so-you-wanna-be-a-beekeeper/.

Page, Autumn. "Detroit Hives Have All the Buzz." *Oakland (University) Post* (Rochester,
MI), February 9, 2021. https://oaklandpostonline.com/34548/features/detroit-hives
-have-all-the-buzz/.

Native Bees and Other Pollinators

Han, Andrew P. "This Bee Buzzes for Blueberries." *Science Friday*, May 13, 2014. https:/www
.sciencefriday.com/articles/picture-of-the-week-this-bee-buzzes-for-blueberries/.

Kopec, Kelsey, and Lori Ann Burd. "Pollinators in Peril: A Systematic Status Review of North
American and Hawaiian Native Bees." *Center for Biological Diversity* (2017). https://
biologicaldiversity.org/campaigns/native_pollinators/pdfs/Pollinators_in_Peril.pdf.

Osterloff, Emily. "Flies Are Saving Your Chocolate Cravings." Natural History Museum. Accessed May
11, 2021. https://www.nhm.ac.uk/discover/flies-are-saving-your-chocolate-cravings.html.

Rodomsky-Bish, Becca. "Do Honey Bees Compete with Native Bees?" Habitat Network, October 18, 2018. https://content.yardmap.org/learn/honey-bees-compete-native-bees/.

U.S. Forest Service. "Pollinator of the Month." Accessed May 11, 2021. https://www.fs.fed.us/wildflowers/pollinators/pollinator-of-the-month/index.shtml.

Honeybees and People

"Colony Collapse Disorder." United States Environmental Protection Agency. Accessed May 11, 2021. https://www.epa.gov/pollinator-protection/colony-collapse-disorder#why%20it%20is%20happening.

Goodrich, Brittney. "A Bee Economist Explains Honey Bees' Vital Role in Growing Tasty Almonds." *The Conversation*, August 29, 2018. https://theconversation.com/a-bee-economist-explains-honey-bees-vital-role-in-growing-tasty-almonds-101421.

Horn, Tammy. *Bees in America: How the Honey Bee Shaped a Nation.* Lexington: University Press of Kentucky, 2006.

McAfee, Allison. "The Problem with Honey Bees." *Scientific American*, November 4, 2020. https://www.scientificamerican.com/article/the-problem-with-honey-bees/.

Electricity and Electric Sensing

American Museum of Natural History. "To Hunt, the Platypus Uses Its Electric Sixth Sense." AMNH blog, January 12, 2021. https://www.amnh.org/explore/news-blogs/news-posts/to-hunt-the-platypus-uses-its-electric-sixth-sense.

Benningfield, Damond. "Ampullae of Lorenzini." *Science and the Sea*, May 1, 2011. https://www.scienceandthesea.org/program/201105/ampullae-lorenzini.

Costandi, Moheb. "How the Ghost Knifefish Became the Fastest Electrical Discharger in the Animal Kingdom." *Science*, March 27, 2018. https://www.sciencemag.org/news/2018/03/how-ghost-knifefish-became-fastest-electrical-discharger-animal-kingdom.

Klein, Joanna. "You're a Bee. This Is What It Feels Like." *New York Times*, December 2, 2016. https://www.nytimes.com/interactive/2016/12/02/science/bees-pollen-senses.html.

Neal, Meghan. "Let's Be Real, Sharks Aren't Eating Google's Undersea Internet Cables." *Vice*, August 14, 2014. https://www.vice.com/en/article/pgazmb/lets-be-real-sharks-arent-eating-googles-undersea-internet-cables.

Chapter 8: Satellite Species

ICARUS and Movebank

Kays, Roland, et. al. "About Movebank." Movebank. Accessed May 11, 2021. https://www.movebank.org/cms/movebank-content/about-movebank.

Maier, Elke. "A Four-Legged Early-Warning System." ICARUS. Accessed May 11, 2021. https://www.icarus.mpg.de/11706/a-four-legged-early-warning-system.

Robbins, Jim. "With an Internet of Animals, Scientists Aim to Track and Save Wildlife." *New York Times*, June 9, 2020. https://www.nytimes.com/2020/06/09/science/space-station-wildlife.html.

Shah, Sonia. "Animal Planet." *New York Times Magazine*, January 12, 2021. https://www.nytimes.com/interactive/2021/01/12/magazine/animal-tracking-icarus.html.

Earthquake Detection

Asendorpf, Leonie. "Can Cows Predict Earthquakes? Animal Observation as an Early Warning System." Translated by Mark Newton. OCHA reliefweb. September 9, 2020. https://reliefweb.int/report/world/can-cows-predict-earthquakes-animal-observation-early-warning-system.

Wikelski, Martin, and Uschi Müller. "The Sixth Sense of Animals: An Early Warning System for Earthquakes?" Max-Planck-Gesellschaft, July 03, 2020. https://www.mpg.de/15126191/earthquakes-animals.

Animal Tracking

Cheshire, James, and Oliver Uberti. *Where the Animals Go: Tracking Wildlife with Technology in 50 Maps and Graphics*. New York: Norton, 2017.

Goldfarb, Ben. "A Space Elk Named Monique." *The Last Word on Nothing*, April 20, 2020. https://www.lastwordonnothing.com/2020/04/20/a-space-elk-named-monique/.

"Introduction to Radio-Telemetry and Wildlife Tracking." Yellowstone Grizzly Project. Accessed May 11, 2021. http://www.yellowstonegrizzlyproject.org/radio-telemetry-and-wildlife-tracking.html.

Yin, Steph. "Inside the Animal Internet." *Silica*, May 20, 2018. https://www.silicamag.com/features/inside-the-animal-internet.

SOURCE NOTES

Chapter 1: Detector Dogs
p. 10: "Those are the fantastic samples" and "I dream of poop like that": author interview with Deborah Giles.

Chapter 2: Fast Ferrets
p. 30: "My ferrets would trade . . . liver paste": author interview with James McKay.

Chapter 4: Gobbling Goats
p. 60: "You put enough goats . . . competition": author interview with Johnny Gonzales.

Chapter 5: First-Alert Fish
p. 72: "there's no test to say . . . toxic or not": author interview with David Trader.

p. 75: "kind of like couch potatoes": ibid.

p. 77: "steady as a rock": ibid.

p. 81: "hero birds": quoted in "Wee Feathered Songsters Give Valuable Assistance to Miners," *Indianapolis Star*, June 20, 1921.

p. 81: "probably the most valuable . . . Bureau ever had": Universal News Service, "Veteran Canary 'Baldy', Hero of Many Mine Explosions, Is Victim of Role as Rescuer," *Star Tribune*, June 26, 1921.

Chapter 6: Dynamite Dolphins
p. 92: "All the dolphins are a little . . . good at": author interview with Jaime Bratis.

p. 99: "A dolphin can do this . . . than a second": author interview with Mark Xitco.

Chapter 7: Community-Building Bees
p. 107: "How about we try . . . bee farm?": author interview with Tim Paule.

p. 113: "a habitat for all living things . . . is thriving": ibid.

Chapter 8: Satellite Species
p. 120: "all the mice and martens . . . other creature": Claudius Aelian, *On the Characteristics of Animals,* vol. 2, trans. A. F. Scholfield (Cambridge, MA: Harvard University Press, 1959), 387.

p. 122: "We call them wearables for wildlife": author interview with Martin Wikelski.

p. 126: "make this sixth sense": ibid.

p. 129: "a good pre-warning": ibid.

BIBLIOGRAPHY

"About Us." Detroit Hives. Accessed May 11, 2021. https://detroithives.org/about-us/.

Aelian, Claudius. *His Various History*. Translated by Thomas Stanley. London, England: Thomas Dring, 1665. http://penelope.uchicago.edu/aelian/.

―――. *On the Characteristics of Animals*, vol. 2. Translated by A. F. Scholfield. Cambridge, MA: Harvard University Press, 1959.

"African Elephant." *National Geographic*. Accessed September 5, 2020. https://www.nationalgeographic.com/animals/mammals/facts/african-elephant.

Agricultural Research Services. "ARS Honey Bee Health." U.S. Department of Agriculture, February 5, 2021. https://www.ars.usda.gov/oc/br/ccd/index/#research.

Allatt, H. T. W. "The Use of Pigeons as Messengers in War and the Military Pigeon Systems of Europe." *Royal United Services Institution Journal* 30, no. 133 (1886): 107–148. https://doi.org/10.1080/03071848609416366.

"Amamigunto National Park Efforts." Government of Japan, Ministry of the Environment. Accessed March 21, 2021. https://www.env.go.jp/en/nature/nps/park/amami/effort.html.

American Museum of Natural History. "To Hunt, the Platypus Uses Its Electric Sixth Sense." AMNH blog, January 12, 2021. https://www.amnh.org/explore/news-blogs/news-posts/to-hunt-the-platypus-uses-its-electric-sixth-sense.

Asendorpf, Leonie. "Can Cows Predict Earthquakes? Animal Observation as an Early Warning System." Translated by Mark Newton. OCHA reliefweb. September 9, 2020. https://reliefweb.int/report/world/can-cows-predict-earthquakes-animal-observation-early-warning-system.

Atema, J. "Structures and Functions of the Sense of Taste in the Catfish (*Ictalurus natalis*)." *Brian, Behavior and Evolution* 4, no. 4 (1971): 273–294. https://www.karger.com/Article/Abstract/125438.

Au, Whitlow W. L. "History of Dolphin Biosonar Research." *Acoustics Today* 11, no. 4 (Fall 2015): 11–17. https://acousticstoday.org/wp-content/uploads/2015/11/Dolphin-Biosonar-Research.pdf.

Au, Whitlow W. L., and James A. Simmons. "Echolocation in Dolphins and Bats." *Physics Today* 60, no. 9. (2007): 40. https://doi.org/10.1063/1.2784683.

Balcombe, Jonathan. *What a Fish Knows: The Inner Lives of Our Underwater Cousins*. New York: Scientific American/Farrar, Straus, and Giroux, 2016.

Barrie, David, and Neil Gower. *Supernavigators: Exploring the Wonders of How Animals Find Their Way*. New York: Experiment, 2020.

Beck, Frank. "Felicia Helps Out." *Fermilab News*, October 5, 2016. https://news.fnal.gov/2016/10/felicia-helps-out.

Beem, Heather R., and Michael S. Triantafyllou. "Wake-Induced 'Slaloming' Response Explains Exquisite Sensitivity of Seal Whisker-like Sensors." *Journal of Fluid Mechanics* 783 (2015): 306–22. doi:10.1017/jfm.2015.513.

Benningfield, Damond. "Ampullae of Lorenzini." *Science and the Sea*, May 1, 2011. https://www.scienceandthesea.org/program/201105/ampullae-lorenzini.

Berman, Tali S. "How Goats Avoid Ingesting Noxious Insects While Feeding." *Scientific Reports* 7, no. 14835 (November 1, 2017). https://doi.org/10.1038/s41598-017-14940-6.

Berta, A., et al. "Eye, Nose, Hair, and Throat: External Anatomy of the Head of a Neonate Gray Whale (Cetacea, Mysticeti, Eschrichtiidae)." *Anatomical Record: Advances in Integrative Anatomy and Evolutionary Biology* 298, no. 4 (2015): 648–659. https://doi.org/10.1002/ar.23112.

Biro, Dora. "Homing Pigeons." *Current Biology* 28, no. 17 (2018): R966–R967. https://doi.org/10.1016/j.cub.2018.05.009.

Blackburn, Tim M., Céline Bellard, and Anthony Ricciardi. "Alien versus Native Species as Drivers of Recent Extinctions." *Frontiers in Ecology and the Environment* 17, no. 4 (May 2019): 203–207. https://doi.org/10.1002/fee.2020.

Blechman, Andrew D. *Pigeons: The Fascinating Saga of the World's Most Revered and Reviled Bird.* St. Lucia: University of Queensland Press, 2007.

"Bluegill." U.S. Fish and Wildlife Service. Accessed April 1, 2021. https://www.fws.gov/fisheries/freshwater-fish-of-america/bluegill.html.

Braczkowski, Alexander Richard. "Curious Kids: Why Do Tigers Have Whiskers?" *The Conversation*, April 4, 2019. https://theconversation.com/curious-kids-why-do-tigers-have-whiskers-110791.

Breithaupt, Thomas, and Petra Eger. "Urine Makes the Difference: Chemical Communication in Fighting Crayfish Made Visible." *Journal of Experimental Biology* 205, no. 9 (2002): 1221–1231. https://doi.org/10.1242/jeb.205.9.1221.

"Brooks Falls Brown Bears." Explore.org. Accessed May 11, 2021. https://explore.org/livecams/brown-bears/brown-bear-salmon-cam-brooks-falls.

Brothers, J. Roger, and Kenneth J. Lohmann. "Evidence that Magnetic Navigation and Geomagnetic Imprinting Shape Spatial Genetic Variation in Sea Turtles." *Current Biology* 28, no. 8 (2018): 1325–1329. https://doi.org/10.1016/j.cub.2018.03.022.

Cagle, Susie. "'Fire Is Medicine': The Tribes Burning California Forests to Save Them." *Guardian*, November 21, 2019. https://www.theguardian.com/us-news/2019/nov/21/wildfire-prescribed-burns-california-native-americans.

Cane, Jim. "Squash Bees." U.S. Forest Service. Accessed May 11, 2021. https://www.fs.fed.us/wildflowers/pollinators/pollinator-of-the-month/squash_bees.shtml.

Cappucci, Matthew. "A Freak Fire Tornado Warning Was Issued in California Saturday amid Swarm of Spinning Blazes." *Washington Post*, August 16, 2020. https://www.washingtonpost.com/weather/2020/08/16/california-fire-tornado-warning.

Carlson, Richard W. "The Influence of pH, Dissolved Oxygen, Suspended Solids or Dissolved Solids upon Ventilatory and Cough Frequencies in the Bluegill *Lepomis macrochirus* and Brook Trout *Salvelinus fontinalis*." *Environmental Pollution Series A, Ecological and Biological* 34, no. 2 (1984): 149–169. https://doi.org/10.1016/0143-1471(84)90055-2.

"Catfish Taste Receptors." North Dakota Game and Fish Department. Accessed October 15, 2020. https://gf.nd.gov/wildlife-notes/catfish-taste-receptors.

"Center for Conservation Biology." University of Washington Center for Conservation Biology. Accessed October 10, 2020. https://conservationbiology.uw.edu.

"Cher Ami." Smithsonian Institution, National Museum of Natural History. Smithsonian ID no. AF.30714, accession no. 65695. https://www.si.edu/object/nmah_425415.

Chernetsov, Nikita et al. "Migratory Eurasian Reed Warblers Can Use Magnetic Declination to Solve the Longitude Problem." *Current Biology* 27, no. 17 (2017): 2647–2651. https://doi.org/10.1016/j.cub.2017.07.024.

Chesapeake Bay Gateways Network. "Monocacy Scenic River Water Trail Map & Guide." https://frederickcountymd.gov/DocumentCenter/View/1275/Monocacy-River-Water-Trail-Map--Guide?bidId=.

Cheshire, James, and Oliver Uberti. *Where the Animals Go: Tracking Wildlife with Technology in 50 Maps and Graphics*. New York: Norton, 2017.

Clarke, Dominic, et al. "Detection and Learning of Floral Electric Fields by Bumblebees." *Science* 340, no. 6128 (2013): 66–69. https://doi.org/10.1126/science.1230883.

Clites, Benjamin L., and Jonathan T. Pierce. "Identifying Cellular and Molecular Mechanisms for Magnetosensation." *Annual Review of Neuroscience* 40 (2017): 231–250. https://doi.org/10.1146/annurev-neuro-072116-031312.

Coen, Jon. "Is the Famed Great White Shark, Mary Lee, Gone Forever?" *Men's Journal*. Accessed May 11, 2021. https://www.mensjournal.com/adventure/is-the-famed-great-white-shark-mary-lee-gone-forever/.

"Colony Collapse Disorder." United States Environmental Protection Agency. Accessed May 11, 2021. https://www.epa.gov/pollinator-protection/colony-collapse-disorder#why%20it%20is%20happening.

Corney, Charlotte. "Why Do Cats Have Whiskers?" *Science Focus*. Accessed September 29, 2020. https://www.sciencefocus.com/nature/why-do-cats-have-whiskers.

Costandi, Moheb. "How the Ghost Knifefish Became the Fastest Electrical Discharger in the Animal Kingdom." *Science*, March 27, 2018. https://www.sciencemag.org/news/2018/03/how-ghost-knifefish-became-fastest-electrical-discharger-animal-kingdom.

Couch, Christina. "The COVID-19 Slowdown Will Show Whether Quieter Seas Help Killer Whales." *Smithsonian*, June 29, 2020. https://www.smithsonianmag.com/science-nature/quieter-seas-covid-19-killer-whales-180975177/.

———. "These Super Rare Butterflies Thrive on Army Bases. The U.S. Military Is Helping Them." *NOVA Next*, April, 17, 2019. https://www.pbs.org/wgbh/nova/article/butterflies-department-of-defense.

Craven, Brent A., Eric G. Paterson, and Gary S. Settles. "The Fluid Dynamics of Canine Olfaction: Unique Nasal Airflow Patterns as an Explanation of Macrosomia." *Journal of the Royal Society Interface* 7, no. 47 (2009): 933–943. doi: 10.1098/rsif.2009.0490.

Cromer, Casey and Mike Neary. "Digestive System and Nutrient Needs of Meat Goats." Purdue Extension. https://extension.purdue.edu/extmedia/AS/AS-628-W.pdf.

Dash, Mike. "Closing the Pigeon Gap." *Smithsonian*, April 17, 2012. https://www.smithsonianmag.com/history/closing-the-pigeon-gap-68103438/.

Davidson, Keay. "Anti-terror Fish Guard S.F.'s Water / Bluegill Monitored to Detect an Attack on City's Drinking Supply." *SFGate*, September 6, 2006. https://www.sfgate.com/news/article/Anti-terror-fish-guard-S-F-s-water-Bluegill-2553021.php.

Davis, Kathleen, and Ira Flatow. "So You Wanna Be a Beekeeper?" *Science Friday*, April 2, 2021. https://www.sciencefriday.com/segments/so-you-wanna-be-a-beekeeper/.

De Brabandere, Sabine. "What Do You Hear Underwater?" *Scientific American*, June 27, 2019. https://www.scientificamerican.com/article/what-do-you-hear-underwater.

Denchak, Melissa. "Water Pollution: Everything You Need to Know." National Resource Defense Council, May 14, 2018. https://www.nrdc.org/stories/water-pollution-everything-you-need-know.

Dewan, Angela, and Max Blau. "Italy Earthquake: 6.6-Magnitude Tremor Rocks Nation's Center." CNN, October 30, 2016. https://www.cnn.com/2016/10/30/europe/italy-earthquake/index.html.

Diemand, Melissa, ed. "2020 Potomac River Report Card." Potomac Conservancy, October 20, 2020. https://potomacreportcard.org/.

"Dissolved Oxygen and Water." USGS. Accessed April 1, 2021. https://www.usgs.gov/special-topic/water-science-school/science/dissolved-oxygen-and-water?qt-science_center_objects=0#qt-science_center_objects.

Drake, Summer E., et al. "Sensory Hairs in the Bowhead Whale, *Balaena mysticetus* (Cetacea, Mammalia)." *Anatomical Record: Advances in Integrative Anatomy and Evolutionary Biology* 298, no. 7 (2015): 1327–1335. https://doi.org/10.1002/ar.23163.

Drummond, R., and R. Carlson. "Procedures for Measuring Cough (Gill Purge) Rates of Fish." U.S. Environmental Protection Agency, 2004. Accessed April 1, 2021. https://cfpub.epa.gov/si/si_public_record_Report.cfm?Lab=NHEERL&dirEntryId=34340.

el-Showk, Sedeer. "An Example of Convergent Evolution in Whales and Bats." *Scitable* (blog). Nature Education, July 1, 2013. https://www.nature.com/scitable/blog/accumulating-glitches/an_example_of_convergent_evolution.

Entwisle, John. "Paul Julius Reuter's Startup: From Brussels to Aix." Thomson Reuters blog, July 20, 2016. https://web.archive.org/web/20190711113431/https://blogs.thomsonreuters.com/answerson/reuters-startup-brussels-aix/.

Erbe, Christine, et al. "The Effects of Ship Noise on Marine Mammals—A Review." *Frontiers in Marine Science* 6 (October 11, 2019). https://doi.org/10.3389/fmars.2019.00606.

Erzurumlu, Reha S., and Patricia Gaspar. "How the Barrel Cortex Became a Working Model for Developmental Plasticity: A Historical Perspective." *Journal of Neuroscience* 40, no. 34 (August 19, 2020). https://www.jneurosci.org/content/40/34/6460.

Eschner, Kat. "This New Zealand Island's Pigeon Mail Stamps Are Still Prized." *Smithsonian*, November 1, 2017. https://www.smithsonianmag.com/smart-news/new-zealand-islands-pigeon-mail-stamps-are-still-prized-180965342/.

Evans, David H., Peter M. Piermarini, and Keith P. Choe. "The Multifunctional Fish Gill: Dominant Site of Gas Exchange, Osmoregulation, Acid-Base Regulation, and Excretion of Nitrogenous Waste." *Physiological Reviews* 85, no. 1 (2005): 97–177. https://doi.org/10.1152/physrev.00050.2003.

Faturechi, Robert, Megan Rose, and T. Christian Miller. "Iran Has Hundreds of Naval Mines. U.S. Navy Minesweepers Find Old Dishwashers and Car Parts." ProPublica, August 5, 2019. https://www.propublica.org/article/iran-has-hundreds-of-naval-mines-us-navy-minesweepers-find-old-dishwashers-car-parts.

Frazier, Katharine. "The History of Bird Banding, Part II." National Audubon Society. Accessed May 11, 2021. https://nc.audubon.org/news/history-bird-banding-part-ii.

Füller, Eva, Ute Kowalski, and Roswitha Wiltschko. "Orientation of Homing Pigeons: Compass Orientation vs Piloting by Familiar Landmarks." *Journal of Comparative Physiology* 153, no. 1 (1983): 55–58. https://doi.org/10.1007/bf00610342.

"Fun Facts about Luscious Lobsters." National Oceanic and Atmospheric Administration Fisheries, September 13, 2019. https://www.fisheries.noaa.gov/national/outreach-and-education/fun-facts-about-luscious-lobsters.

Gabriel, Larry. "Detroit's Vacant Lot Problem." *Detroit Metro Times*, June 6, 2018. https://www.metrotimes.com/detroit/detroits-vacant-lot-problem/Content?oid=12700362.

Gale Ambassadors. "Canaries in the Coal Mine." *The Gale Review* (blog). Gale International, September 8, 2020. https://review.gale.com/2020/09/08/canaries-in-the-coal-mine/.

Giaimo, Cara. "France's Lost Pigeon-and-Balloon Memorial Is Well Worth Remembering." *Atlas Obscura*, November 16, 2017. http://www.atlasobscura.com/articles/pigeon-balloon-memorial-paris-bartholdi.

Giaimo, Cara. "The Surprisingly Sticky Tale of the Hadza and the Honeyguide Bird." *Atlas Obscura*, February 17, 2016. https://www.atlasobscura.com/articles/the-surprisingly-sticky-tale-of-the-hadza-and-the-honeyguide-bird.

Gilliland, Haley Cohen. "A Brief History of the US Navy's Dolphins." *MIT Technology Review*, October 24, 2019. https://www.technologyreview.com/2019/10/24/306/dolphin-echolocation-us-navy-war.

Gillis, J. Andrew, and Olivia R. A. Tidswell. "The Origin of Vertebrate Gills." *Current Biology* 27, no. 5 (2017): 729–732. https://doi.org/10.1016/j.cub.2017.01.022.

Glick, Molly. "What Makes a Firenado?" *Sierra*, August 25, 2020. https://www.sierraclub.org/sierra/what-makes-firenado.

"Global Songbird Migration." ICARUS. Accessed May 11, 2021. https://www.icarus.mpg.de/31292/black_birds.

Goldfarb, Ben. "A Space Elk Named Monique." *The Last Word on Nothing*, April 20, 2020. https://www.lastwordonnothing.com/2020/04/20/a-space-elk-named-monique/.

Goodrich, Brittney. "A Bee Economist Explains Honey Bees' Vital Role in Growing Tasty Almonds." *The Conversation*, August 29, 2018. https://theconversation.com/a-bee-economist-explains-honey-bees-vital-role-in-growing-tasty-almonds-101421.

Gordon, Iain J., and Herbert H. T. Prins. "Browsers and Grazers Drive the Dynamics of Ecosystems." In *The Ecology of Browsing and Grazing*, vol. 2, 405–445. Berlin: Springer, 2019. https://doi.org/10.1007/978-3-030-25865-8_16.

Gotfredson, David, and Steve Price. "Grayfish: Video Exposes Navy Dolphin Care on San Diego Bay." CBS8, April 27, 2017. https://www.cbs8.com/article/news/grayfish-video -exposes-navy-dolphin-care-on-san-diego-bay/509-b2a33153-0662-472f-ac51 -3703e47f7746.

Grant, Robyn. "How We Found a Special Maths Equation Hidden in Rat Whiskers." *The Conversation*, January 27, 2020. https://theconversation.com/how-we-found -a-special-maths-equation-hidden-in-rat-whiskers-130345.

Grant, Robyn A., et al. "The Evolution of Active Vibrissal Sensing in Mammals: Evidence from Vibrissal Musculature and Function in the Marsupial Opossum *Monodelphis domestica*." *Journal of Experimental Biology* 216, no. 18 (September 2013). https://doi.org/10.1242 /jeb.087452.

Gray, Irving Emery. "Comparative Study of the Gill Area of Marine Fishes." *Biological Bulletin* 107, no. 2 (1954): 219–225. https://doi.org/10.2307/1538608.

"Great Barrier Island Pigeongram Agency: Mail Form 9." Museum of New Zealand. Registration no. GH006251. https://collections.tepapa.govt.nz/object/286960.

"Green Invaders." *National Geographic Kids*. Accessed October 14, 2020. https://kids .nationalgeographic.com/science/article/green-invaders.

Greenfieldboyce, Nell. "Inuit Hunters Help Scientists Track Narwhals." NPR, August 19, 2009. https://www.npr.org/2009/08/19/111980557/inuit-hunters-help-scientists-track -narwhals.

Greenwood, Veronique. "This Parasite Doesn't Need Oxygen to Survive." *New York Times*, February 28, 2020. https://www.nytimes.com/2020/02/28/science/parasite-oxygen -mitochondria.html.

Gross, Rachel E. "Some Historically Fueled Guesses on What Russia Will Do With Its War Dolphins." *Slate*, March 28, 2016. https://slate.com/technology/2016/03/a-short-history -of-war-dolphins.html.

Grüner, Tamara. "Radio Collars Stress Vulnerable Voles." *Nature*, February 28, 2005. https://www.nature.com/news/2005/050228/full/news050228-3.html.

Guerra, Patrick A., Robert J. Gegear, and Steven M. Reppert. "A Magnetic Compass Aids Monarch Butterfly Migration." *Nature Communications* 5, no. 4164 (2014): 1–8. https://doi .org/10.1038/ncomms5164.

Han, Andrew P. "This Bee Buzzes for Blueberries." *Science Friday*, May 13, 2014. https://www .sciencefriday.com/articles/picture-of-the-week-this-bee-buzzes-for-blueberries/.

Hand, Eric. "Maverick Scientist Thinks He Has Discovered a Magnetic Sixth Sense in Humans." *Science*, June 23, 2016. https://www.sciencemag.org/news/2016/06 /maverick-scientist-thinks-he-has-discovered-magnetic-sixth-sense-humans.

Handwerk, Brian. "In Some Ways, Your Sense of Smell Is Actually Better Than a Dog's." *Smithsonian*, May 22, 2017, https://www.smithsonianmag.com/science-nature /you-actually-smell-better-dog-180963391.

Harley, Heidi E., Erika A Putman, and Herbert L Roitblat. "Bottlenose Dolphins Perceive Object Features through Echolocation." *Nature* 424 (2003): 667–669. https://doi .org/10.1038/nature01846.

Hecker, Bruce. "How Do Whales and Dolphins Sleep Without Drowning?" *Scientific American*, February 2, 1998. https://www.scientificamerican.com/article/how-do-whales-and-dolphin.

Hofmann, R. R. "Evolutionary Steps of Ecophysiological Adaptation and Diversification of Ruminants: A Comparative View of Their Digestive System." *Oecologia* 78 (1989): 443–457. https://link.springer.com/content/pdf/10.1007/BF00378733.pdf.

Hooper, Rowan. "Sperm Whale's Emergency Evacuation . . . of Its Bowels." *New Scientist*, January 28, 2015. https://www.newscientist.com/article/mg22530064-700-sperm-whales-emergency-evacuation-of-its-bowels.

Horn, Tammy. *Bees in America: How the Honey Bee Shaped a Nation.* Lexington: University Press of Kentucky, 2006.

Horowitz, Alexandra. *Being a Dog: Following the Dog into a World of Smell.* New York: Scribner, 2016.

"How Does a Bluegill Act Like a Canary?" Blue Sources. Accessed April 1, 2021. https://www.bluesources.com/#about.

"How Dolphins Steer Their Sonar." *Science*, March 18, 2009. https://www.sciencemag.org/news/2009/03/how-dolphins-steer-their-sonar.

"Indigenous Peoples Burning Network." Nature Conservancy Conservation Gateway. Accessed May 10, 2021. http://www.conservationgateway.org/ConservationPractices/FireLandscapes/Pages/IPBN.aspx.

Inscoe, Michael. "The Pigeon Express." *Atlas Obscura*, September 29, 2017. https://www.atlasobscura.com/places/pigeon-express.

"Introduction to Radio-Telemetry and Wildlife Tracking." Yellowstone Grizzly Project. Accessed May 11, 2021. http://www.yellowstonegrizzlyproject.org/radio-telemetry-and-wildlife-tracking.html.

"Invasive Non-Native Species." U.S. Environmental Protection Agency. Accessed October 14, 2020. https://www.epa.gov/watershedacademy/invasive-non-native-species.

Jerolmack, Colin. *The Global Pigeon.* Chicago: University of Chicago Press, 2013.

Kays, Roland, et. al. "About Movebank." Movebank. Accessed May 11, 2021. https://www.movebank.org/cms/movebank-content/about-movebank.

Khan, Amina. "Like a Tree's Rings, Blue Whale's Earwax Tells a Story of Its Life." *Los Angeles Times*, September 18, 2013. https://www.latimes.com/science/sciencenow/la-xpm-2013-sep-18-la-sci-sn-blue-whale-ear-wax-plug-pollutants-hormones-20130916-story.html.

Kimchi, Tali, Ariane S. Etienne, and Joseph Terkel. "A Subterranean Mammal Uses the Magnetic Compass for Path Integration." *Proceedings of the National Academy of Sciences* 101, no. 4 (2004): 1105–1109. https://doi.org/10.1073/pnas.0307560100.

King, Stephanie L., et al. "Vocal Copying of Individually Distinctive Signature Whistles in Bottlenose Dolphins." *Proceedings of the Royal Society B* 280, no. 1757 (April 22, 2013). https://doi.org/10.1098/rspb.2013.0053.

King, Stephanie L., and Vincent M. Janik. "Bottlenose Dolphins Can Use Learned Vocal Labels to Address Each Other." *Proceedings of the National Academy of Sciences* 110, no. 32 (2013): 13216–13221. https://doi.org/10.1073/pnas.1304459110.

Klein, JoAnna. "Magnetic Sense Helps Billions of Moths on an Australian Migration." *New York Times*, June 21, 2018. https://www.nytimes.com/2018/06/21/science/moths-magnetic -australia.html.

———. "You're a Bee. This Is What It Feels Like." *New York Times*, December 2, 2016. https://www.nytimes.com/interactive/2016/12/02/science/bees-pollen-senses.html.

Kopec, Kelsey, and Lori Ann Burd. "Pollinators in Peril: A Systematic Status Review of North American and Hawaiian Native Bees." Center for Biological Diversity, February 2017. https://biologicaldiversity.org/campaigns/native_pollinators/pdfs/Pollinators_in _Peril.pdf.

Kuhnlein, Harriet V., and Murray M. Humphries. "Moose." Centre for Indigenous Peoples' Nutrition and Environment. Accessed May 11, 2021. http://traditionalanimalfoods.org /mammals/hoofed/page.aspx?id=6132.

Kuklina, Iryna, Antonín Kouba, and Pavel Kozák. "Real-Time Monitoring of Water Quality Using Fish and Crayfish as Bio-indicators: A Review." *Environmental Monitoring and Assessment* 185, no. 6 (2013): 5043–5053. https://doi.org/10.1007/s10661-012-2924-2.

Langley, Liz. "Echolocation Is Nature's Built-in Sonar. Here's How It Works." *National Geographic*, February 3, 2021. https://www.nationalgeographic.com/animals/article /echolocation-is-nature-built-in-sonar-here-is-how-it-works.

Laplander, Robert. "Finding the Lost Battalion: Myths and Legends." Internet Archive. Accessed May 11, 2021. https://web.archive.org/web/20190126001115/https://www .theirownmemorial.org/index.php/finding-the-lost-battalion-myths-and-legends.html.

Lee, Christopher. "Bluegill on Guard in Region's Water Supply." *Washington Post*, September 18, 2006. https://www.washingtonpost.com/archive/politics/2006/09/18/bluegill-on -guard-in-regions-water-supply/e6331e99-e447-49a8-b329-fd3a572c1966/.

Leffer, Lauren. "These Mighty Shorebirds Keep Breaking Flight Records — And You Can Follow Along." *Audubon*, October 8, 2021. https://www.audubon.org/news /these-mighty-shorebirds-keep-breaking-flight-records-and-you-can-follow-along.

Little, Becky. "Early Humans May Have Scavenged More than They Hunted." History Channel website, January 9, 2020. https://www.history.com/news/prehistoric-human -diet-scavengers-vs-hunters.

"Lobsters Pee Out of Where?" *New England Aquarium Exhibit Galleries* (blog), November 13, 2015. http://galleries.neaq.org/2015/11/lobsters-pee-out-ofwhere.html.

López-Uribe, Margarita M., James H. Cane, Robert L. Minckley, and Bryan N. Danforth. "Crop Domestication Facilitated Rapid Geographical Expansion of a Specialist Pollinator, the Squash Bee *Peponapis pruinosa*." *Proceedings of the Royal Society B: Biological Sciences* 283, no. 1833 (2016): 1–9. https://doi.org/10.1098/rspb.2016.0443.

"M 6.6 – 7 km N of Norcia, Italy." USGS, Latest Earthquakes. Accessed May 11, 2021. https://earthquake.usgs.gov/earthquakes/eventpage/us1000731j/executive.

Madsen, Peter T., et al. "Nasal Sound Production in Echolocating Delphinids (*Tursiops truncatus* and *Pseudorca crassidens*) Is Dynamic, but Unilateral: Clicking on the Right Side and Whistling on the Left Side." *Journal of Experimental Biology* 216, no. 21 (2013): 4091– 4102. https://doi.org/10.1242/jeb.091306.

"Magnetoreception." Lohmann Lab, University of North Carolina at Chapel Hill. Accessed May 12, 2021. https://lohmannlab.web.unc.edu/magnetoreception/.

Mahdy, Mohamed A. A., Salma A. Mohamed, and Kamal E. H. Abdalla. "Morphological Investigations on the Lips and Cheeks of the Goat (*Capra hircus*): A Scanning Electron and Light Microscopic Study." *Microscopy Research & Technique* 83, no. 9 (September 2020): 1095–1102. https://doi.org/10.1002/jemt.23500.

Maier, Elke. "A Four-Legged Early-Warning System." ICARUS. Accessed May 11, 2021. https://www.icarus.mpg.de/11706/a-four-legged-early-warning-system.

Man, John. Saladin: *The Sultan Who Vanquished the Crusaders and Built an Islamic Empire*. Boston, MA: Da Capo, 2016.

Mancini, Mark. "15 Incredible Facts about Pigeons." *Mental Floss*, April 19, 2018. https://www.mentalfloss.com/article/535506/facts-about-pigeons.

Manson, Bill. "Controlling Wildfires the Native American Way." *San Diego Reader*, August 19, 2020. https://www.sandiegoreader.com/news/2020/aug/19/golden-dreams-controlling-wildfires-native.

Marsh, Alison. "Consider the Pigeon, a Surprisingly Capable Technology." *IEEE Spectrum*, March 29, 2019. https://spectrum.ieee.org/tech-history/silicon-revolution/consider-the-pigeon-a-surprisingly-capable-technology.

Marshall, Michael. "Zoologger: Pink Magnet Slug Doesn't Need Ruby Slippers." *New Scientist*, July 7, 2011. https://www.newscientist.com/article/dn20662-zoologger-pink-magnet-slug-doesnt-need-ruby-slippers/.

Martini, Sabine, Sabine Begall, Tanja Findeklee, Marcus Schmitt, E. Pascal Malkemper, and Hynek Burda. "Dogs Can Be Trained to Find a Bar Magnet." *PeerJ* 6 (2018): e6117. https://doi.org/10.7717/peerj.6117.

Maryland Department of the Environment Water Management Administration Water Supply Program. "Source Water Assessment for Fort Detrick Water Treatment Plant." May 2005. https://mde.state.md.us/programs/Water/water_supply/Source_Water_Assessment_Program/Documents/www.mde.state.md.us/assets/document/watersupply/SWAPS/Frederick/Fort%20Detrick%20Water%20Treatment%20Plant.pdf.

McAfee, Allison. "The Problem with Honey Bees." *Scientific American*, November 4, 2020. https://www.scientificamerican.com/article/the-problem-with-honey-bees/.

McGann, John P. "Poor Human Olfaction Is a 19th-Century Myth." *Science* 356, no. 6338 (May 12, 2017). https://science.sciencemag.org/content/356/6338/eaam7263.

McIntosh, Alan, and William Bishop. *Distribution and Effects of Heavy Metals in a Contaminated Lake*. West Lafayette: Purdue University, 1976. Accessed April 1, 2021. https://www.arlis.org/docs/vol1/C/726432558.pdf.

McKie, Robin. "Humans Hunted for Meat 2 Million Years Ago." *Guardian*, September 22, 2012. https://www.theguardian.com/science/2012/sep/23/human-hunting-evolution-2million-years.

"Medical Detection Dogs." Medical Detection Dogs. Accessed March 21, 2021. https://www.medicaldetectiondogs.org.uk.

Micu, Alexandru. "In Poznan, Poland, Eight Clams Get to Decide If People in the City Get Water or Not." ZME Science, December 28, 2020. https://www.zmescience.com/science/poznan-mussel-water-plants-892524/.

Moisset, Beatriz. "Yucca Moths (*Tegeticula* sp.)." U.S. Forest Service. Accessed May 11, 2021. https://www.fs.fed.us/wildflowers/pollinators/pollinator-of-the-month/yucca_moths .shtml.

Moisset, Beatriz, and Vicki Wojcik. "The Alkali Bee (*Nomia melanderi*)." U.S. Forest Service. Accessed May 11, 2021. https://www.fs.fed.us/wildflowers/pollinators/pollinator-of-the -month/alkali_bee.shtml.

Mongilio, Heather. "Frederick Company to Expand on Fort Detrick Fish Biomonitoring System." *Frederick (MD) News-Post*, March 2, 2019. https://www.fredericknewspost .com/news/science_and_technology/frederick-company-to-expand-on-fort-detrick-fish -biomonitoring-system/article_9c7780ec-c553-53fc-9ea4-cb607d6dd120.html.

Morell, Virginia. "Ancient Humans Hunted Monkeys for Tens of Thousands of Years." *Science*, February 19, 2019. https://www.sciencemag.org/news/2019/02/ancient-humans -hunted-monkeys-tens-thousands-years.

———. "Dolphins Can Call Each Other, Not by Name, But by Whistle." *Science*, February 20, 2013. https://www.sciencemag.org/news/2013/02/dolphins-can-call -each-other-not-name-whistle.

Moulton, D. G., G. Celebi, and R. P. Fink. "Olfaction in Mammals—Two Aspects: Proliferation of Cells in the Olfactory Epithelium and Sensitivity to Odours." In *Taste and Smell in Vertebrates*, edited by G. E. W. Wolstenholme and Julie Knight, 227–250. London: Churchill, 1970.

Munz, Martin, Michael Brecht, and Jason Wolfe. "Active Touch During Shrew Prey Capture." *Frontiers in Behavioral Neuroscience* 4, no. 191 (December 2010). https://doi.org/10.3389 /fnbeh.2010.00191.

"*Mustela putorius furo*—The 'Smelly Thief.'" University of Wisconsin-La Crosse BioWeb. Accessed October 31, 2020. http://bioweb.uwlax.edu/bio203/s2014/ziglioli_andr /classification.htm.

Neal, Meghan. "Let's Be Real, Sharks Aren't Eating Google's Undersea Internet Cables." *Vice*, August 14, 2014. https://www.vice.com/en/article/pgazmb/lets-be-real-sharks-arent -eating-googles-undersea-internet-cables.

Newman, Andy. "2,000 Pigeons Will Put on a Light Show in Brooklyn." *New York Times*, April 28, 2016. https://www.nytimes.com/2016/04/29/arts/design/-duke-riley-pigeons-fly -by-night.html.

Noack, Rick. "Estonia Is Still Clearing Thousands of World War II Mines from Its Waters." *Washington Post*, October 26, 2018. https://www.washingtonpost.com/world/2018/10/26 /estonia-mines.

Nuwer, Rachel. "This Catfish's Whiskers Are Like Ultra-Sensitive pH Strips." *Smithsonian*, June 5, 2014. https://www.smithsonianmag.com/science-nature/catfish-whiskers-are -ultra-sensitive-ph-strips-180951665/.

Osoro, K., et al. "Diet Selection and Performance of Sheep and Goats Grazing on Different Heathland Vegetation Types." *Small Ruminant Research* 109, (2013): 119–127.

Osterloff, Emily. "Flies Are Saving Your Chocolate Cravings." Natural History Museum. Accessed May 11, 2021. https://www.nhm.ac.uk/discover/flies-are-saving-your -chocolate-cravings.html.

Padnani, Amy. "Anatomy of Detroit's Decline." *New York Times*, December 8, 2013. https://archive.nytimes.com/www.nytimes.com/interactive/2013/08/17/us/detroit-decline.html.

Page, Arthur W., ed. *The World's Work: A History of Our Time*. Vol. 28. Garden City, NJ: Doubleday, Page, 1914.

Page, Autumn. "Detroit Hives Have All the Buzz." *Oakland (University) Post* (Rochester, MI), February 9, 2021. https://oaklandpostonline.com/34548/features/detroit-hives-have-all-the-buzz/.

Palmer, Brian. "How Long Can You Hold Your Breath?" *Slate*, November 18, 2013. https://slate.com/technology/2013/11/nicholas-mevoli-freediving-death-what-happens-to-people-who-practice-holding-their-breath.html.

Parker, Joe, et al. "Genome-wide Signatures of Convergent Evolution in Echolocating Mammals." *Nature* 502 (2013): 228–231. https://doi.org/10.1038/nature12511.

Penn, Ivan, Peter Eavis, and James Glanz. "How PG&E Ignored Fire Risks in Favor of Profits." *New York Times*, March 18, 2019. https://www.nytimes.com/interactive/2019/03/18/business/pge-california-wildfires.html.

Perras, Michael, and Silke Nebel. "Satellite Telemetry and Its Impact on the Study of Animal Migration." *Nature Education Knowledge* 3, no. 4 (2012).

Peterson, Todd. "Homing Pigeons." *BirdNote*. https://www.birdnote.org/listen/shows/homing-pigeons.

Pettigrew, John D. "Electroreception in Monotremes." *Journal of Experimental Biology* 202, no. 10 (1999): 1447–1454.

Pierre-Louis, Kendra, and John Schwartz. "Why Does California Have So Many Wildfires?" *New York Times*, June 16, 2021. https://www.nytimes.com/article/why-does-california-have-wildfires.html.

Pinkowski, Jen. "Why Physicists Tried to Put a Ferret in a Particle Accelerator." *Atlas Obscura*, April 2, 2019. https://www.atlasobscura.com/articles/felicia-ferret-particle-accelerator-fermilab.

Pochron, Sharon. "By a Whisker." *Science News for Students*, September 2, 2012. https://www.sciencenewsforstudents.org/article/whisker.

Povoledo, Elisabetta. "Italy, Already Rattled, Is Struck by Another Powerful Quake." *New York Times*, October 30, 2016. https://www.nytimes.com/2016/10/31/world/europe/italy-earthquake-norcia.html.

"Protected Areas for Antelopes." ICARUS. Accessed May 11, 2021. https://www.icarus.mpg.de/31598/saiga-antelopes.

Raeburn, Paul. "Sharks Attack Sophisticated Undersea Telephone Cable." Associated Press News, August 21, 1986. https://apnews.com/article/5e1b697fbb64f479b524d237d3471bd1.

Reep, R. L., et al. "Distribution and Innervation of Facial Bristles and Hairs in the Florida Manatee (*Trichechus manatus latirostris*)." *Marine Mammal Science* 14, no. 2 (April 1998). https://doi.org/10.1111/j.1748-7692.1998.tb00715.x.

"RMA Pigeon Story." *Rocky Mountain Adventures*, February 22, 2021. https://www.shoprma.com/articles/rma-pigeon-story/.

Robbins, Jim. "With an Internet of Animals, Scientists Aim to Track and Save Wildlife." *New York Times*, June 9, 2020. https://www.nytimes.com/2020/06/09/science/space-station-wildlife.html.

Rodomsky-Bish, Becca. "Do Honey Bees Compete with Native Bees?" Habitat Network, October 18, 2018. https://content.yardmap.org/learn/honey-bees-compete-native-bees/.

Romero, Ezra David. "How Indigenous Burning Practices Could Prevent Massive Wildfires." *Science Friday*, September 25, 2020. https://www.sciencefriday.com/segments/indigenous-fire-prevention.

Rose, Naomi A., E. C. M. Parsons, and Richard Farinato. "The Case Against Marine Mammals in Captivity." Humane Society of the United States and World Society for the Protection of Animals, 2009. Accessed January 15, 2021. https://www.humanesociety.org/sites/default/files/docs/case-against-marine-captivity.pdf.

Russell, Karen. "Monocacy Is Not a Healthy River." *Frederick (MD) News-Post*, September 23, 2017. https://www.fredericknewspost.com/opinion/letter_to_editor/monocacy-is-not-a-healthy-river/article_2707510e-b76c-5c4b-a6ac-aa639e9a8258.html.

Sabar, Ariel. "A Military Base's Last Line of Toxic Defense: Bluegills." *Baltimore Sun*, January 20, 2003. https://www.baltimoresun.com/news/bs-xpm-2003-01-20-0301200188-story.html.

Sarko, Diana K., Frank L. Rice, and Roger L. Reep. "Mammalian Tactile Hair: Divergence from a Limited Distribution." *Annals of the New York Academy of Sciences* 1225 (April, 2011): 90–100.

Schmidt-Koenig, Klaus, and Charles Walcott. "Tracks of Pigeons Homing with Frosted Lenses." *Animal Behaviour* 26, no. 2 (1978): 480–486. https://doi.org/10.1016/0003-3472(78)90065-9.

Schmitt, Melissa H., David Ward, and Adam M. Shrader. "Salivary Tannin-Binding Proteins: A Foraging Advantage for Goats?" *Livestock Science* 234 (April 2020). https://doi.org/10.1016/j.livsci.2020.103974.

"Scientific Contributions of the US Navy Marine Mammal Program 2020." Naval Information Warfare Center Pacific (NWIC Pacific). Accessed January 15, 2021. https://www.niwcpacific.navy.mil/wp-content/uploads/2021/03/Scientific-Contributions-US-Navy-Marine-Mammal-Program2020.docx.

Shah, Sonia. "Animal Planet." *New York Times Magazine*, January 12, 2021. https://www.nytimes.com/interactive/2021/01/12/magazine/animal-tracking-icarus.html.

Shedd, Tommy R., W. H. van der Schalie, M. W. Widder, D. T. Burton, and E. P. Burrows. "Long-Term Operation of an Automated Fish Biomonitoring System for Continuous Effluent Acute Toxicity Surveillance." *Bulletin of Environmental Contamination and Toxicology* 66, no. 3 (2001): 392–399. https://doi.org/10.1007/s001280018.

Shen, Yong-Yi, et al. "Parallel Evolution of Auditory Genes for Echolocation in Bats and Toothed Whales." *PLOS Genetics* (June 28, 2012). https://doi.org/10.1371/journal.pgen.1002788.

Shimojo, Shinsuke, Daw-An Wu, and Joseph Kirschvink. "Humans Can Sense Earth's Magnetic Field, Brain Imaging Study Says." *Discover*, March 18, 2019. https://www.discovermagazine.com/planet-earth/humans-can-sense-earths-magnetic-field-brain-imaging-study-says.

Small, Dana. "How Does the Way Food Looks or Its Smell Influence Taste?" *Scientific American*, April 2, 2008. https://www.scientificamerican.com/article/experts-how-does-sight-smell-affect-taste.

Society for Neuroscience. "Fish Talk-os: Studying Electrocommunication in the Wild." Phys.org, May 7, 2018. https://phys.org/news/2018-05-fish-talk-os-electrocommunication-wild.html.

"Species Directory: Killer Whale." National Oceanic and Atmospheric Administration Fisheries. Accessed November 22, 2020. https://www.fisheries.noaa.gov/species/killer-whale#spotlight.

Spencer, Erin. "How Do Gills Work?" *Ocean Currents* (blog). Ocean Conservancy, January 17, 2020. https://oceanconservancy.org/blog/2020/01/17/gills/.

"State Area Measurements and Internal Point Coordinates." United States Census Bureau, August 9, 2018. https://www.census.gov/geographies/reference-files/2010/geo/state-area.html.

Steinbring, Scot. "Wildland Fire Program." Karuk Tribe official website. Accessed May 10, 2021. https://www.karuk.us/index.php/departments/natural-resources/eco-cultural-revitalization/wildland-fire-program.

Stetka, Bret. "Seals Use Their Whiskers to See and Hear." *Atlantic*, October 30, 2015. https://www.theatlantic.com/science/archive/2015/10/seals-use-their-whiskers-to-see-and-hear/413269.

Stookesberry, Ben. "Pigeon Express." *Vimeo*, July 29, 2018. https://vimeo.com/5558263.

"Stop the Trafficking." Africa Wildlife Foundation. Accessed March 21, 2020. https://www.awf.org/stop-trafficking.

"The Story of the Navy Dolphins." *Frontline*. Accessed June 1, 2020. https://www.pbs.org/wgbh/pages/frontline/shows/whales/etc/navycron.html.

Sundstrom, Bob. "Canary in a Coal Mine." *Birdnote*, July 2017. https://www.birdnote.org/listen/shows/canary-coal-mine.

Sutton, Gregory P., Dominic Clarke, Erica L. Morley, and Daniel Robert. "Mechanosensory Hairs in Bumblebees (*Bombus terrestris*) Detect Weak Electric Fields." *Proceedings of the National Academy of Sciences* 113, no. 26 (2016): 7261–7265. https://doi.org/10.1073/pnas.1601624113.

Sweeney, Don. "Glass Fire Burned 1 Acre Every 5 Seconds in California. How Fast Can Wildfires Grow?" *Sacramento Bee*, September 29, 2020. https://www.sacbee.com/news/california/fires/article246092930.html.

"Tannins." U.S. Forest Service. Accessed June 3, 2021. https://www.fs.fed.us/wildflowers/ethnobotany/tannins.shtml.

"10 Interesting Things about Air." NASA. Accessed April 1, 2021. https://climate.nasa.gov/news/2491/10-interesting-things-about-air/.

"Tiny Ferret Aids Construction of Nat Meson Lab." *Village Crier* (National Accelerator Laboratory newsletter) 3, no. 35 (September 2, 1971). https://history.fnal.gov/criers/9-2-1971.pdf.

"Top 20 Largest California Wildfires." Cal Fire, April 28, 2021. https://www.fire.ca.gov/media/4jandlhh/top20_acres.pdf.

Trumble, Stephen J., et al. "Blue Whale Earplug Reveals Lifetime Contaminant Exposure and Hormone Profiles." *Proceedings of the National Academy of Sciences* 110, no. 42 (October 15, 2013): 16922–16926. https://doi.org/10.1073/pnas.1311418110.

Turturici, Armando Alessandro. "China Across Sea in Early Ming Dynasty—The Figure of Zheng He 1." *Quarterly Journal of Chinese Studies 4*, no. 3 (2016): 111–114. https://search.proquest.com/docview/1804471515?pq-origsite=gscholar&fromopenview=true.

Tyson, Peter. "Dogs' Dazzling Sense of Smell." *NOVA*, October 4, 2012. https://www.pbs.org/wgbh/nova/article/dogs-sense-of-smell.

Uberti, Oliver. "Where the Wild Things Go." *Nautilus*, August 17, 2017. https://nautil.us/issue/51/limits/where-the-wild-things-go.

Universal News Service. "Veteran Canary 'Baldy,' Hero of Many Mine Explosions, Is Victim of Role as Rescuer." *Star Tribune* (Minneapolis), June 26, 1921.

U.S. Forest Service. "Pollinator of the Month." Accessed May 11, 2021. https://www.fs.fed.us/wildflowers/pollinators/pollinator-of-the-month/index.shtml.

"U.S. Navy Marine Mammal Program." Naval Information Warfare Center Pacific (NWIC Pacific), Accessed July 22, 2020. https://www.niwcpacific.navy.mil/marine-mammal-program.

Valle, Shelley. "How Do We Sense Taste?" Arizona State University, *Ask a Biologist*, October 6, 2017. https://askabiologist.asu.edu/smell-taste.

van der Schalie, Bill. "Aquatic Biomonitoring for Rapid, Continuous Toxicity Assessment." PowerPoint presentation, U.S. Army Center for Environmental Research, August 25, 2004. https://www.potomacdwspp.org/Meetings/Aug25-2004/van_der_Shalie_%20biomonitoring.pdf.

Walcott, Charles. "Pigeon Homing: Observations, Experiments and Confusions." *Journal of Experimental Biology* 199, no. 1 (1996): 21–27. https://jeb.biologists.org/content/jexbio/199/1/21.full.pdf.

Walker, Dianne Beidler. et al. "Naturalistic Quantification of Canine Olfactory Sensitivity." *Applied Animal Behaviour Science* 97, nos. 2–4 (2006): 241–254.

Wang, Kelin, Qi-Fu Chen, Shihong Sun, and Andong Wang. "Predicting the 1975 Haicheng Earthquake." *Bulletin of the Seismological Society of America* 96, no. 3 (2006): 757–795. https://doi.org/10.1785/0120050191.

"Water Treatment." Centers for Disease Control and Prevention. Accessed April 1, 2021. https://www.cdc.gov/healthywater/drinking/public/water_treatment.html.

"Wee Feathered Songsters Give Valuable Assistance to Miners." *Indianapolis Star*, June 20, 1921.

"What Is Sonar?" National Oceanic and Atmospheric Administration, National Ocean Service, updated February 26, 2021. https://oceanservice.noaa.gov/facts/sonar.html.

Whelan, Bob, and Sue Kempf. "Wildfire Mitigation and Fire Safety Report." City of Laguna Beach. July 2019. https://www.lagunabeachcity.net/civicax/filebank/blobdload.aspx?t=71727.78&BlobID=22875.

Wieskotten, S., et al. "Hydrodynamic Determination of the Moving Direction of an Artificial Fin by a Harbour Seal (*Phoca vitulina*)." *Journal of Experimental Biology* 213, no.13 (July 2010). https://doi.org/10.1242/jeb.041699.

Wikelski, Martin, and Uschi Müller. "The Sixth Sense of Animals: An Early Warning System for Earthquakes?" Max-Planck-Gesellschaft. July 03, 2020. https://www.mpg.de/15126191/earthquakes-animals.

Wikelski, Martin, Uschi Mueller, Paola Scocco, Andrea Catorci, Lev V. Desinov, Mikhail Y. Belyaev, Daniel Keim, Winfried Pohlmeier, Gerhard Fechteler, and P. Martin Mai. "Potential Short-Term Earthquake Forecasting by Farm Animal Monitoring." *Ethology* 126, no. 9 (2020): 931–941. https://doi.org/10.1111/eth.13078.

Wisniewska, Danuta M., et al. "Range-Dependent Flexibility in the Acoustic Field of View of Echolocating Porpoises (*Phocoena phocoena*)." *eLife.* (2015). https://elifesciences.org/articles/05651.

Woodcock, T. S. "Pollination in the Agricultural Landscape: Best Management Practices for Crop Pollination." *University of Guelph: Canadian Pollination Initiative (NSERC-CANPOLIN)* (2012). http://seeds.ca/pollinator/bestpractices/images/Pollination%20in%20Agricultural%20Landscape_Woodcock_Final.pdf.

"Working Ferrets." National Ferret School. Accessed October 30, 2020. https://ferretbusiness.honeybank.com/working-ferrets.

Yee, Amy. "How These Dogs Protect Elephants." *National Geographic*, April 27, 2016, https://www.nationalgeographic.com/animals/article/160427-kenya-wildlife-service-sniffer-dogs-smuggled-ivory-airport-port-elephant-poaching.

Yin, Steph. "Inside the Animal Internet." *Silica*, May 20, 2018. https://www.silicamag.com/features/inside-the-animal-internet.

Yong, Ed. "Echolocation in Bats and Whales Based on Same Changes to Same Gene." *National Geographic*, January 25, 2010. https://www.nationalgeographic.com/science/article/echolocation-in-bats-and-whales-based-on-same-changes-to-same-gene.

———. "The History of the Oceans Is Locked in Whale Earwax: The Massive Plugs Contain Spikes and Dips of Stress Hormones that Perfectly Match the History of Modern Whaling." *Atlantic*, November 21, 2018, https://www.theatlantic.com/science/archive/2018/11/astonishing-history-locked-whale-earwax/576349.

Zeldovich, Lina. "The Great Dolphin Dilemma." *Hakai*, February 5, 2019. https://www.hakaimagazine.com/features/the-great-dolphin-dilemma.

ACKNOWLEDGMENTS

Special thanks to the animal handlers, researchers, and other experts who generously gave their time for interviews, fact-checking, consultation, and animal fairness reads.

Detective Dogs

Dr. Deborah Giles, killer whale biologist at the University of Washington's Center for Conservation Biology • Dr. Monica Mansfield, veterinarian at Medway Animal Hospital • Dr. Andy Roark, veterinarian and host of the YouTube show *Cone of Shame*

Dynamite Dolphins

Jaime Bratis, marine mammal scientist at the US Navy Marine Mammal Program at the Naval Information Warfare Center Pacific (NIWC Pacific) • Jim Fallin, director of Corporate Communications and Public Affairs at the US Navy Marine Mammal Program • Dr. James Finneran, research scientist at the US Navy Marine Mammal Program • Dr. Frants Jensen, behavioral ecologist at the Woods Hole Oceanographic Institution • Dr. Aude Pacini, marine mammal scientist at the University of Hawaii's Marine Mammal Research Program • Dr. Mark Xitco, director of the US Navy Marine Mammal Program

Special Delivery Pigeons

Dr. Dora Biro, animal behavior zoologist at the University of Oxford • David Costlow, former owner of Rocky Mountain Adventures • Dr. Salima Ikram, Distinguished University Professor of Egyptology at the American University in Cairo • Dr. Richard Redding, archeozoologist at Ancient Egypt Research Associates • Dr. Nigel Spivey, senior lecturer in Classics at the University of Cambridge • David Terry, co-owner of Rocky Mountain Adventures • Dr. Ross Thomas, curator of Greek and Roman collections at the British Museum

Gobbling Goats

Dr. Christopher Dicus, professor of wildland fire and fuels management at California Polytechnic State University • Dr. Zen Faulkes, biologist at McMaster University • Johnny Gonzales, owner of Environmental Land Management • Dr. Homero Salinas-Gonzalez, state extension and research specialist in small ruminants at Lincoln University •

Dr. Andrea Watson, research associate professor of ruminant nutrition at the University of Nebraska–Lincoln

First-Alert Fish

Terry Collins, owner of Blue Sources • Dr. Joanne Parrot, fish biologist at the Water Science and Technology Directorate, Environment and Climate Change Canada • David Trader, US Army biologist • Melissa Diemand, senior director of communications at the Potomac Conservancy

Fast Ferrets

Lauren Biron, Fermilab Office of Communication • Dr. Robyn Grant, senior lecturer in comparative physiology and behavior at Manchester Metropolitan University • Valerie Higgins, archivist at Fermilab • James McKay, zoologist and director of the National Ferret School • Dr. Olivia Petritz, assistant professor of avian and exotic animal medicine at North Carolina State University • Dr. Miranda Sadar, assistant professor of avian, exotic, and zoological medicine at Colorado State University

Community-Building Bees

Nicole Lindsey, co-founder and co-owner of Detroit Hives • Dr. Felicity Muth, professor of animal cognition at the University of Texas at Austin • Tim Paule, co-founder and co-owner of Detroit Hives • Dr. Daniel Robert, professor of bionanoscience at the University of Bristol • Dr. Lila Westreich, graduate researcher at the University of Washington

Satellite Species

Sarah Davidson, data curator at Movebank • Sabine Knopf, assistant to the director at the Max Planck Institute of Animal Behavior • Ben Goldfarb, science writer • Dr. Martin Wikelski, professor at the Max Planck Institute of Animal Behavior

Other Material

Dr. Dolly Jørgensen, environment and technology historian and professor of history at the University of Stavanger • Brandon Keim, science writer

We are extremely grateful to Amy Brand and Bill Smith at MIT Press, to Karen Lotz at Candlewick Press, and to the fabulous editorial and design team we worked with, especially Hilary Van Dusen and Olivia Swomley, who were so generous with their time and expertise, and Rachel Wood, who made the book look great. Additional thanks to Ana Facciolo, Alan Lightman, Margaret Czerwienski, Kate Petersen, Leah Butler, Joelle Riffle, and Marc Haeringer, who all lent their time and help, and to our families—Lilia Kilburn; Deb Gfeller; Mike Giaimo; Mari Giaimo; Tori, Ben, and Tyler Todd; Linda Call; and Jason and Lillian Adams—for tolerating our relentless stream of weird animal facts.

IMAGE CREDITS

INDEX

PAGE NUMBERS IN ITALIC REFER TO AN IMAGE AND/OR CAPTION TEXT.
PAGES IN ROMAN TYPE MAY ALSO INCLUDE RELEVANT IMAGES AND/OR CAPTIONS.

CHRISTINA COUCH AND CARA GIAIMO are science journalists and alums of the MIT Graduate Program in Science Writing. Christina Couch writes about the wonderful weirdness of brains (organic and artificial), and Cara Giaimo writes about the amazing lives of animals. You can find their work in the *New York Times*, *Wired*, and *Atlas Obscura*, on *NOVA*, and in other outlets.

DANIEL DUNCAN is the author-illustrator of *South* and the illustrator of *Mr. Posey's New Glasses* by Ted Kooser, *The Girl Who Could Fix Anything* by Mara Rockliff, and *The Purple Puffy Coat* by Maribeth Boelts. Daniel Duncan creates most of his work in an old stable turned studio on the outskirts of London.